EVERYMAN TODAY CALL ROME

# EVERYMAN TODAY CALL ROME

## By Charles A. Coulombe

*Charlemagne Press   Arcadia*

ISBN 0-944455-00-X
Library of Congress Catalog
Card Number 87-72184

Second Edition
April 1988

*To the memory of James Francis Cardinal McIntyre;*

*To the Alumni, Cadets, Faculty, and Staff of
New Mexico Military Institute; and*

*To my dear parents, Guy and Patricia Coulombe;*

*This Book is lovingly dedicated.*

## ACKNOWLEDGMENTS

For the completion of this book, special thanks are due, out of an enormous number of people, to the following:

Mrs. Donald Schabow, for typing and endless typing; Mr. Neil Citrin, for editing the manuscript; Mr. Charl Van Horn, for teaching me the craft of writing; Br. Leonard Mary, MICM, Stephan, Baron Hoeller-Bertram, and Mr. Ryan Brookhart, for their ideas and encouragement; Mr. Tom Zola, for his practical assistance; my brother, Andre N. Coulombe; and all my dear friends, whose lives and experience inspired this effort.

Brief quotations from the following are gratefully acknowledged: Rev. Charles E. Coughlin, *Bishops versus the Pope;* Rev. Paul Crane, SJ, "Christian Order;" Rev. Peter Geiermann, *The Convert's Catechism of Christian Doctrine;* C.G. Jung, *The Symbolic Life;* Don Gaspar Le Febvre, *The St. Andre Missal;* Dom Charles Poulet, *A History of the Catholic Church;* The Slaves of the Immaculate Heart of Mary, *Our Glorious Popes;* R. Emmett Tyrell, Jr. *The Liberal Crack-Up.*

# Contents

# 1 - EMBATTLED LEGACY

# A Case of Robbery

We have been robbed. By "we" I mean those Catholics born after 1956. By "robbed," I mean raised with little or no understanding or knowledge of Catholic doctrine, practice, or heritage. What does it mean to be a Catholic in the 1980's? Why are we not Protestants? How are we different? Does it matter? And most of all, why were we not told the answers to these questions by priests, nuns, or our parents? We will try to find some solution to these problems and, coincidentally, include some tips on rebuilding Catholicity in a hostile environment.

To start with, we must take stock of ourselves. Since we are all going to die, and since the time spent dead is much longer than that spent alive, it follows that our religion, our Church, must be the most important thing in our lives. Is it? Are we more concerned with securing eternal happiness, or with temporary pleasure? Will an MBA from a really good business school provide salvation? Is possession of high grade cocaine a plus in the day of judgment? If you answer affirmatively, then you will pardon my preaching and proceed to heaven via Club Med.

For those of us left behind, the question remains: How necessary to us is our religion? The litmus question is this - would we die for it? Could we, like St. Thomas More, sacrifice everything in its defense? If the answer is yes, the question becomes "why?" If no, it is time to join our Club Med-bound brethren.

The "why" here is most important.

The most common perceptions of the Church today are either that it is a very wealthy and flawed organization which is somehow important, or (for the more devout) that it is the assembly of believers gathered together to celebrate the Lord's Supper and hear the word of God. This last is very nice, doubtless, but I would find it very hard to die for either idea. Really, it would be too much to put off a ball game, let alone die, for the Church. Luckily, neither is true.

The first definition is held by those individuals who are misinformed about the history of the Church, and about human psychology. While Christ did not appoint Monsignori, or prescribe the shape of the host, he didn't sit under a tree expecting his teachings to be maintained through racial memory, either. In the setting aside of Peter, and the delineation of apostles versus regular disciples, we see the main outlines of the hierarchy of today. If Christ saw fit to establish a structure, He must have had a reason. He was God, after all. One might say, then, that the Church is worth our attention and study, at very least, if He put so much time into its creation. A manufacturing company in existence under the same management since the time of the Roman empire would excite our interest, so why not the Church?

The second definition is partly true, and thus much more destructive. One assumes that the reader of this book is sincerely interested in his religion or, he would not have picked up the book. And having perhaps been active in his local parish, parochial school, or Confraternity of Christian Doctrine, this is the definition he has most likely been taught. But it is only a part of the truth. It is as misleading on its own as being taught that the U.S.A. is merely the strip of land separating Mexico from the Dominion of Canada. The concomitance of that teaching—that priests are merely presidents of the worshipping assembly with no quasi-"magical" powers of transubstantiation; that the eucharist is merely a memorial of the Last Supper; that all forms and doctrines are changeable according to the whims of the day; that the Pope is merely the chief bishop, and the papacy is optional in any case; and worst of all, that truth is dependent upon man's understanding, rather than God's will—is not merely Protestant or Modernist, but satanic. If you assault the teachings of God's church, you assault God. And the wages of that sin are certainly death. What is truly inexplicable is why people would reject the filet mignon of Catholicism for the Big Mac of pseudo-Catholicism. Yet this is what a large part of the generation of Catholics which preceded us have done. Still, what is one to expect from the generation who brought us Mood Rings and Pet Rocks?

To truly understand the extent of the damage done to the Catholic Church as a human institution, we must examine what wreckage is left from the attempt of our fathers and elder brothers to remake the Church in their own, admittedly somewhat tacky, image. If you can obtain a pre-1960 missal, one of the things that will strike you is the mystery, the depth, of the liturgy described there. A detailed and complete missal is a very good guide to authentic Catholicism, and is uncommonly good literature as well. But what did the beat generation, in their great haste to be trendy, leave us? A watered down rite that is as uninspiring as it is insipid. What reflection of the glory of God is it? Even a junior high student would know that "All glory and honor *is* yours..." is poor usage. Not content with stealing the majesty and solemnity of the mass, they took its grammar too. Even Luther and Cranmer stopped at that.

This bebop "rebel without a cause" attitude affected every sector of Catholic practice in the 1960's and '70's, and is with us yet. But by trivialising the Church in their care, our predecessors did more than gratify their own egos. They made the Church appear to be less than worth dying for, and thus less than worth living for. And in doing so they lost the greater part of our generation.

In the following pages, we will attempt to put before your eyes some of the now not-so-trendy concepts our aged fathers-in-the-faith propounded, and the truths they abandoned. The time is coming when we young people will hold the Church in our hands. If we are to do our duty to Christ the King, we must accept the challenge of Catholic reconstruction. To do that, we must each of us acquire the education denied us. We could not help being robbed; we can blame only ourselves if we remain poor.

# The Mystical Body

Well then, if the Catholic Church is more than merely the assembly of believers, what is it? There are four facets to its nature which we will discuss. The first of these is that of the Church as the Kingdom of God. The old Covenant of God with Israel established the Jews as the chosen people to bear witness to Him, until the Messiah should come. Sacrifice was the key action on the part of Israel, and around the bloody sacrifice of the Temple, the whole of Hebrew life was centered. The high priest and Aaronic hereditary priesthood who offered it, the king and army who defended it, and the people of the twelve tribes who provided it, existed solely for its sake. As a holy people, a royal priesthood, they lived under a special law, for Yahvah took them as His particular subjects, and He was high king over all kings in Jerusalem. When they strayed from His will, they were punished. Like Jerusalem itself, Israel was a walled city often besieged.

With Christ's coming, all this changed. The Jewish establishment rejected Him (as well they might someone who dared to violate the Sabbath, claimed to forgive sins, threw moneychangers out of the temple, and generally acted as though He owned the place) and eventually killed Him. In a few years the temple was destroyed, the Jewish hierarchy wrecked, and the bloody sacrifice ended. But in place of fallen Israel a new chosen people had been founded, with an unbloody sacrifice born of Christ's own Body and Blood to offer. To His Apostle Peter He gave the high priesthood, and to His other apostles He gave the priesthood of Melchisedek. Where descent had been required for citizenship in the old kingdom of God, discipleship was needed in the new, baptism rather than blood. The new inheritor of the promises of Abraham, the Catholic Church, was born.

In some ways, the Church was much like its prototype: strictly hierarchical, organized around the sacrifice of the Mass, and holding a covenant until the second coming of the Messiah. Thus the Church stands as the inheritor of Israel. In a sense we Catholics are more Jewish than the Jews, for we continue the structure and the mission which they lost when they failed to recognize Christ. The Catholic must always be a bit wistful when he sees the Jew. But for human pride they might both be subjects of the same kingdom, and but for divine grace they might both be outside the gate.

Heaven, therefore is not the only province of the kingdom of God. It truly resides within us in the Church. That is why the Eastern Rites of the Church, (and the Latin Rite, until the time of Little Richard and the Beach Boys) surrounds the sacrifice of the Mass, and even the building in which it is offered up, with mystery and splendor. Icons, statues, lights, candles, incense, chanting, and noble, unchanging language are employed to give one a foretaste of Heaven. The rituals of the Church are the royal court ceremonial of God. And if we surround earthly soverigns, who only reflect the authority and power of God, with pomp and glory, how much more solemn and splendid should be the homage given their prototype?

The next facet to look at is that of the Mystical Body of Christ. Here is where the real magic comes in, for this is no empty phrase. The Church continues the work of her founder in the same manner that He would if He were present in an obvious physical form. She teaches the same doctrines, and dispenses the same care that He did. In particular, She regularly performs seven miracles, which He performs through her priests and bishops, as He did through the first Apostles. In baptism, He and She blot out the sin of Adam, and add souls to the Mystical Body. In confirmation, the Holy Ghost proceeds to inflame the individual soul, as He did at Pentecost. Christ forgives sins in an immediate fashion at confession, and heals at extreme unction. He makes more apostles at ordination. Best of all, He appears, Body and Blood, humanity and divinity, as a sacrificial victim, at every Mass. Thus does the hierarchy of the Church act in union with Him. It even unites two souls in matrimony, which only He can do. The sacraments act as the life blood of the Church, constantly reviving and strenghthening the most remote of her members. But, as with a physical body, lack of blood means loss of limb. We must continue in that stream if we wish to remain part of Him.

What of us, the successors of the disciples? When we obey the authentic authority of his Church, we obey Him. When we remind our erring brethren of their duty, spread His Catholic truth, give a good example in our own lives, assist the needy, and comfort each other in adversity, we are doing His work. As laymen, we have an obligation to study our faith, in these days when priests, nuns and bishops often seem to have abandoned it to follow the gospel according to Jane Fonda.

Our Protestant Fundamentalist friends often accuse us of being unbiblical. (Of course, they often claim that alcohol is sinful, which would have doubtless shocked Our Lord at Cana!) But the third facet which we will examine is the Church as the custodian of the Bible. Before 393 A.D., when the Church codified the canon of the Bible, there were many books floating around, all of them supposed to be written by one apostle or another. The early Church looked to apostolic tradition, as embodied in the living witness of their successors, the Pope and the bishops. Since the Gospels were meant for edification, they were read and profited by. But as St. John 21:25 tells us, not everything that Christ did (or taught) was in them. After the Church put the Bible in its present form, she continued to interpret it. At the Reformation, the Protestants dropped those parts of the Bible they found offensive. But even so they could not answer the problem posed by the passage in St. Matthew 16:18: "Thou art Peter (Rock) and upon this Rock I will build my Church and the gates of Hell shall not prevail against it. And I will give unto thee the keys of the Kingdom of Heaven. Whatsoever thou shalt loose on earth shall be loosed in Heaven." If the Church founded on Peter the Rock is wrong, then the gates of Hell did prevail, and Christ was a liar. If She is right, then Peter's successor, the Pope, still holds the keys to the kingdom.

When we take these three facets as a whole, they add up to the fourth; the Church is the gate of salvation. We are told in the Gospel that no man reaches the Father save through Christ. We are told further that Christ does not know those who cast out devils in his name, but without his authority. We are told by the Bible, by tradition, and by a long line of councils and popes, that one who belongs to the Church will lose his soul if he leaves it, and might even if he doesn't. We are nowhere given assurance that non-Catholics can go to Heaven. There is only one way there that we know of, and if it is painful to think of our many virtuous non-Catholic friends being lost, we should double our efforts to teach them the Faith. If we are true friends, we will try to share our greatest treasure with those we love. Christ never said that one could be saved by being nice, and claimed to bring not peace but a sword. There are many priests who would perhaps say otherwise. One must reply: "But Father, if I can be saved as easily outside the Church as in her, why bother? Especially as your sermons are boring and you always ask me for money."

There she is then, the new Jerusalem covered with tin foil, the human mixed with the divine. But she is a city, and history tells us that occasionally those who should guard her gates let outside evils come in. This evidently is what our Pepsi-generation clerics did. Despite their efforts, however, a little digging reveals that she is still the Mystical Body of Christ. She is not only worth dying for, she is eminently worth living for.

# Unending Sacrifice

We must now speak about the Mass. As it is the center of Catholic life, we can assume that it is a good barometer of the depth of Catholic practice. First, we must define it. We will quote Dom Gaspar Lefebvre, O.S.B.'s introduction to the *St. Andre* Missal:

> The worship addressed by the Church to the Father through Christ takes the form both of *sacrifice* and of *prayer*.
>
> *Sacrifice* is the highest form of liturgical worship, that which most fully recognises His sovereign dominion over creation.
>
> By His bloody sacrifice on the cross, Christ merited for each of us our redemption and the graces necessary to obtain it.
>
> After His resurrection and ascension He continues His priesthood by presenting His glorious wounds before His Father in our favor. On this bloodless Calvary He obtains in heaven the application to our souls of what He merited for us on Golgotha.
>
> At the same time Our Lord applies these same merits to us, even on earth. For this end He has left to His Church an unbloody Sacrifice, which not only represents, but renews, the bloody oblation of Calvary, Holy Mass. The sacrifice is the same, for it is the same Priest and the same victim. Christ is the High Priest; but to perform the rites of this sacrifice, a lower order of Priesthood of Christ are the members of the Catholic Hierarchy, and thus at one

and the same time, by Christ invisible, and by Christ visible, it is ordained that we shall pray to God in the person of the Pope, Bishops, and Priests. These priests are the official intermediaries between heaven and earth. And it is by means of the liturgy we can unite ourselves with the sacerdotal prayer of the Church, and all together day by day by the same rites, the same formulas, even by the same chant, render to our Lord with her a worship worthy of the most High.

Due to transubstantiation we are in the presence of Christ Himself, and the Mass becomes the most transcendental experience a human being can undergo.

Now our Protestant brethren, ever solicitous of biblical purity, will reinterpret the words of Christ in the gospel from "This is My body...This is My blood," to "This is a representation of My body...This is a memorial of My blood." Our Modernist Catholic friends would agree. Our Lord, however, has not seen fit to be guided by their pronouncements, showing the great ignorance of which only a god is capable.

But having established the nature of the gift bestowed upon us, we must now explore our treatment of it. After all, the Eucharist being our greatest treasure, we would naturally treat it with unbounded respect, as the presence of the Eternal King would seem to demand. But do we?

We would receive it kneeling, one would suppose, as befits subjects in the royal court. We would take it upon our tongues, as only the priest's hands are bound up to handle it. But we don't! Not we of the New Age! We move up as in a lunch line, take it in our hand, and chew the Host like hard candy. Very respectful! Most edifying! After all, He is merely our Creator and Saviour. What homage do we owe Him?

It might also be assumed that we would surround the great action with the greatest solemnity and beauty possible. The Church furnishings and the vestments would be the most expensive and intricate we could afford. Incense, holy water and chanting would add to the mystery and majesty. Perhaps we would employ an ancient, unchanging language to emphasize the eternity and universality of the event. But no, *we* know better. God is better served in cold, bare, ugly places with the priest attired in cheap rags. He certainly does not merit the traditional forms with which mankind everywhere has always honored its concept of divinity. Surely his praises ought to be expressed in the most juvenile and mundane manner possible. After all, He is only God!

Of course, I am being slightly facetious. The fact remains, however, that the reforms instituted by the Pepsi generation did not create an upsurge of devotion. Whatever the theory, whatever the justification, they cannot claim that their attempts to renew the liturgy were done out of a desire to reinforce eucharistic piety. If they did it would show that they were not merely ignorant of psychology, but of logic.

Now none of this meant to imply that the new Mass is invalid. The Church is incapable of proclaiming an invalid rite. Indeed, I have seen the new Mass done with devotion, piety, reverence, and respect. But due to its ambiguity, its ceaseless number of options, it lends itself to innumerable annoying variations.

No one has ever proven that the old Mass was not as good as the new. They just proclaimed the new, as though so-called experts were the only members of the Church. But we, the laymen, we of the twenty-first century, are also members. What is more, we are the future; they are a small footnote of the past.

In the immediate, we must work at cultivating devotion to the Blessed Sacrament. In the context of the new Mass, we must receive on the tongue, and kneel to do so. Both are supposed to be within our rights, so let us challenge the priests to deliver. On the other hand, we must agitate for the liberty to hear the old Mass, and work to spread it. After all, Mao-Tse-Tung (to whom some middle-aged priests listen more than to the Pope) said, "Let a hundred flowers bloom... let a hundred schools of thought content." Surely our antiquated liberal clergy would not fear that.

Lastly, we must not fail to visit our Lord in the tabernacle.

Although many parishes have removed Him to a side altar, most have not yet disposed of Him entirely. A visit to Him is always rewarding, even if the local padre finds Donahue's company more exciting. We must keep in mind always that He is a king, even if His own priests and people deny Him. We should say with Thomas Moore "One sword at least, thy right shall guard, one faithful harp shall praise Thee."

Another point that might as well be touched upon here is the psychological aspect. Carl Gustaf Jung, writing in 1939, in a time and place (Switzerland) where the Church was not fearful of itself:

> The fact is that there are relatively few neurotic Catholics; and yet they are living under the same conditions as we do. They are presumably suffering from the same social conditions and so on, and so one should expect a similar amount of neurosis. There must be something in the cult, in the actual religious practice, which explains that peculiar fact that there are fewer complexes, or that these complexes manifest much less in Catholics than in other people. That something, besides confession, is really the cult itself. It is the Mass, for instance. The heart of the Mass contains a living mystery, and that is the thing that works... [1]

Luckily, our bishops have been able to bring us into the modern world, at least as far as allowing us to be as neurotic as our non-Catholic neighbors. But those familiar with the old Mass might also remember the pre-communion prayer of St. Thomas Aquinas, which reads in part..."I approach as one who is sick to the physician of life..." It would be strange indeed if the Eucharist, the Sacrifice of the Mass did not work in that way.

Our modern gurus do not attack the sacrificial and mysterious aspects of the Mass, however. Rather they

1. Jung, C.G. "The Symbolic Life," p.8

overemphasize a lesser, though valid, facet - the Mass as meal. Then, by de-mystifying it, putting the host in the hand, having the congregation troop up to receive, turning round the altar, and purging the language of the Mass from most sacrificial phrasing, the more important aspect is phased out.

Their Eminences, Excellencies, Graces, and Lordships who permitted these things, the monsignori, priests and nuns who carried them out, and the lay folk who stood for them, have much to answer for. But even yet, in every Catholic Church, the great mystery remains. They may treat Him with disrespect, they may attempt to deceive us, but He remains and calls to us, asking for our loyalty.

# A Treasure Hunt

## Baptism

According to *The Convert's Catechism of Catholic Doctrine,* baptism "is a sacrament which frees us from original sin, makes us children of God, brethren of Christ, and co-heirs with Him of the Kingdom of Heaven."[2]

Here, then, in one sacrament, we find the whole plan of salvation. Christ in the gospel ordered it as clearly as He did the Mass. Baptism cleanses us of original sin, and thus accomplishes the goal of regeneration, of restoring us to God's grace. All the sacraments become available to us, and we are incorporated into the Mystical Body of Christ.

It also faces us with a challenge. He bought the right for us to be redeemed with water by His blood. But that gives us the requirement of loyalty to the Church He founded, to believe the precepts He taught. There are no free rides in this world!

Our revered elders, in their dubious wisdom, attempted to do with baptism the same sort of thing they have done with all else, to emphasize the secondary aspect to the exclusion of the primary. In this case, they attempt to mention baptism merely as Christian initiation. (Taking them as examples causes doubt as to the validity of regeneration! Fear not, though; it does exist). To that end they have subtly altered the rite for baptism, removing the exorcisms and generally attempting to remove the "magical" elements. Were it not for that "magic," they would not have the hope of salvation they insist on gambling with.

2. The Convert's Catechism of Catholic Doctrine, Rev. Peter Geiermann, C.SS.R., P. 69

## Confirmation

Here is the forgotten sacrament. It is most often gone through like a Catholic Bar-Mitzvah, as a mere rite-of-passage. But it is more than that. The old catechisms said it was the reception of grace necessary to be a soldier of Christ. And so it is, because all of us, upon maturity, ought to become soldiers of Christ.

At Pentecost, the Holy Ghost came down upon the apostles so that they could preach the Gospel to all nations and carry the war into the enemy camp. They were sent out like lambs among wolves. Well, confirmation is like Pentecost for one. In a sense one becomes an apostle and is given the same charges they were. It is the start of the lifelong struggle that will hopefully lead to salvation not merely for the individual, but for many whom his life touches.

In most professions one may take someone for an inspiration. So too, on entering this career the person takes a saint's name, hoping to emulate the saint and to invoke his intercession. Although many of our priests would like it to be so, John Lennon, Jack Kerouac, and James Dean are not yet on the list.

Before our aged predecessors changed it, the bishop used to give each confirmand a slap on the cheek. This represented the requirement of a soldier of Christ to suffer persecution or death for the Faith if needed. And truly, any one who attempts to practice it will find great difficulty and disquiet, due to internal sin, outside contempt, and general misunderstanding. Confirmation allows one the grace to stand it.

## Penance

Here we come to the real meat of the topic. This is the sacrament concerned with sin. We young moderns, of course, have none. Before the great stupefaction of the 1960's, however, sin was very much a problem. People did all sorts of things. They lied, they cheated, they stole. Some drank, took drugs or gambled, to the detriment of their families, while others cheated on their wives, or selected lovers of the inappropriate sex. Some fornicated while others embezzled, and all had pride, envy, jealousy, and a ton of other little flaws. It was into such a world Our Lord came, and began, upon repentance, to forgive sins. His Church, following His mandate, continued to do so.

Today, due to the realization of self-perfection occuring about the time of Haight-Ashbury and the Summer of Love, many, if not most, Catholics in America have abandoned the practice. It is to be hoped that God will see them as sinless as they see themselves on the day of judgement.

For we poor sinful mortals left here, however, prey to the various amusements just mentioned, confession is the one sure way out of the trap of sin and death. The liberals and the Protestants will say, "Ah, but can't one just pray to God for forgiveness?" Yes, but He did give the apostles His command to forgive sins. And so, when a Catholic confesses his sins with a contrite heart, accepts the penance the priest gives him, and resolves to start anew, then the slate is wiped clean. His guilt must vanish, for the sin has. This, in contrast to our fundamentalist friends, who boast of their lack of need of earthly intermediaries and yet seem to base their religiosity upon fear and guilt.

Let us therefore ignore the revelation given the flower children (now gone to seed), admit our sins, and gladly use the source of life granted us.

## Ordination

We have come now to a prime mystery. The priesthood is a supreme gift, although at times its holders make this difficult to believe. If God were dumb, He would doubtless have committed His word and mission entirely to a book, easy to misinterpret, and unable to defend itself. Since He knew what kind of characters He was dealing with, however, He created a Priesthood. In terms of perfection, it fell short like all things human. In terms of what was possible, it was the best solution.

The Apostles were the first bishops. In creating them thus, Christ instituted the sacrament of Holy Orders. In laying hands upon others and passing on the Episcopate, they began the apostolic succession. Those possessed of it were able to create priests, forgive sins, confirm, marry, baptise, and best of all, perform the sacrifice of the Mass. The priests could not ordain, of course, and did not have the jurisdiction of the apostles. Nevertheless, they did and do have the power to do all else.

To all the pagan nations of antiquity, the concept of the priesthood was an important one. Even they knew that one cannot approach the Godhead, and not be burned. Thus, all of them had one thing in common with the Jews - their priests were hedged about with all sorts of restrictions. Either they were celibate or promiscuous, or they could only marry certain people; they might be selected only from certain families; their training was arduous. The Catholic priesthood is thus a living sacrifice, called by God to offer Himself to Himself.

Many priests, in these new age days, would prefer to relinquish their mystic power. They would rather be presidents of the assembly than offerers of the altar; initiators than baptisers; counselors than confessors. So be it. But let them give up also their salaries and sinecures, their cooks and Cadillacs. If we laymen forced them to consider, the question not in terms of theology but in terms of revenue, orthodoxy would bloom.

## Marriage

This sacrament is, today, one of the most abused. Considering the moral guidance offered by our inebriate fathers, this is perhaps to be understood. Even so, we must educate ourselves, find out the truth, and proceed according to it.

The Church teaches us that marriage is a sacrament ordained by God, which unites two people for the furtherance of their mutual salvation, fulfillment, and happiness, the begetting of children, the formation of a Catholic household, and the strengthening of church and society. The bond is indissoluable. Adultery, abortion and artificial contraception are grave sins which debase marriage.

The alternative to marriage the Church gives us is the celibate life. We may be priests, brothers or nuns, or merely live in the

world in a chaste manner. Sex is reserved to the married state.
Now by this point I will probably have lost most of my readers.
Even if you have persevered with me to this chapter, you will
throw down the book in disgust, if you are older, (doubtless
murmuring, "not that old trash again!"), or else just closing it in
bewilderment, if you are younger. Please do not, fearless reader! I
guarantee that you will appreciate my point later on.

Back to marriage. A great part of our problem as a generation
came from the lack of regard in which our parents held the
married state. When our parents did not see our growth and
formation and each other's happiness as a God-given responsibility, there was the Faith untaught, there were our lives and
loves twisted, there was our moral growth stunted. When our
parents felt our spiritual lives unimportant, they allowed foolish
priests and nuns to mis-teach us unimpeded, or committed our
souls to the public schools. When they were more concerned
with their own pleasures than with their mates' or children's
welfare, they divorced, setting us a fine example. When the
opposite of these things were true, then we knew our Faith, lived
in fairly happy homes, and through their example, learned to be
men and women. Many of us fell between these two poles, of
course. "By their fruits ye shall know them," says the Bible, and
we are the living embodiments of our parent's sins and virtues.

Despite the many jibes at the Church's marital morality, the
fact remains that no great modern thinker, not Camus, not
Sartre, has come up with a better familial system. One look at
our own generation may serve to convince one of that. In the
families where both partners attempt to live up to the
sacramental ideal, to place each other first, to greet each infant as
a divine grace, there happiness will be abundant, and a firm
foundation for life both temporal and eternal may be assured. If
on the other hand, we take the marriage-as-contract stand, then
we have temporary unions lacking stability, dependability or
purpose. We have in fact, sex-on-call. But that is much more
easily accomplished through just living together. After all,

though, it is so much easier living alone. But the fact remains that in marriage as in everything else, the Church must fight against the constant human urge to self-centeredness. People can say that they live only for themselves. If they live that way, they will spend eternity that way. Let him who has eyes to read, read.

## Holy Unction

Now we have hit all the sacraments but one, the one for the sick and the dying. Holy Unction at once brings the healing power of God upon the victim, either restoring him, or else preparing him for death. Given with confession and communion, it places the soul in readiness for Heaven. Here we see the churchly power, the priestly character in full perspective. For the priest will feed you with the Bread of Life, he will absolve you of the evil you have done, and he will anoint you with the oil of divine healing. After you have died, the Church will, in the person of her priests, reach through space, time and death, to apply the merits of Masses to you, and get you from Purgatory much sooner than ever you could yourself. For the love that Christ, and thus the Church, has for you is unending. It will pursue you beyond the grave, and open the Gate of Heaven for you. But you must accept it. You must accept His Mystical Body loyally and obediently. If you and I do this, we will be heirs of the kingdom. If not, we must go to Club Med, and have on earth what we'll miss hereafter.

# II – THEY MEANT WELL
## OR
## LOSS OF HONOR

# Love Among the Ruins

The next section of this little book is about the history of how things got to be in the silly mess that they are in at present. We have seen some of the marvelous truths of the Church in the intro, and some of the erroneous views of "theologians", in this day when the Church seems to have little strength in this world. But it was not always so.

One of the best known writers amongst our generation today is the late Professor J.R.R. Tolkien. Tolkien (a fervent Catholic, several of whose children entered the religious life) wrote a piece called the *Lord of the Rings,* which deals with a faraway region called Middle Earth where elves, hobbits (which he invented), dwarves, and men fought a last-ditch effort against Sauron, the evil Dark Lord of Mordor. Gondor, noblest of the surviving realms of men, had been exhausted by its long struggle with Sauron, its line of kings had failed, and its ruling stewards (who reigned in the King's place) were unable to revive its flagging fortunes. But then...go buy the book. I'm not doing it justice. In any case, the youth of 1960's America fell in love with it. Unfamiliar with folklore and medieval romance (heretofore the property of isolated cultural pockets, immigrants, and literature professors) few of the young literati of the time could resist it. They formed societies, re-enactment groups and study fellowships around it, and the entire fantasy genre mushroomed. The imaginations of millions were fired by tales of sword, sorcery, and daring deeds and rescues. Many sighed imploringly, "if only it were true."

Surprise, friends! I have a true adventure for you. Steeped in bravery, heroism, magic, and mystery, with everything from a truly evil enemy, to ancient brotherhoods, primitive tribes, evil traitors, mistaken do-gooders, and captive peasants. Why, there is even a lady, for whose honour the heroes must live and die. It is of course the story of the Church, in much abbreviated form. Were I to tell you the whole of it, I would tire of writing sooner than you would of reading it.

So, pretend that I am not an author, and you are not reading. Instead, pretend that I am a minstrel, and you a noble, when the King of Gondor sat in Osgiliath, the Citadel of the Stars, before the shadow returned to Mordor.

Every tale of wonder begins with the phrase, "Once upon a time." Generally, the time is not too specific. For our story, though, we do have a time. The thirteenth century may be said to have been the Church's golden age. Saintly messengers and martyrs had spread Christ's rule all over Europe. The century opened with the pontificate of Innocent III, one of the finest vicars of Christ ever to grace the throne of St. Peter. One might describe the Pope and his time in the following manner:

> It is difficult for us in the 20th Century to understand Pope Innocent's extraordinary labor and his influence on the monarchs and governments of the 13th Century. We have been slowly and deliberately taught that monarchies and kings are bad things, and papal supervision of any kind in government, even over its morals, is a *very* bad thing...[3]

> Scarcely anyone is ever told any more that France, Spain and Portugal, Poland and Hungary, England and Sweden, all had kings and queens who were saints, and who ruled their lands gloriously and brought untold happiness and well-being to their subjects.

> No one is told that when great monasteries were to be found on almost every hill in Europe there was never any need of bread lines or soup kitchens, for the hungry could always find food and a night's

> lodging with the monks. It was only with the coming
> of the "Reformation" that poorhouses and poor
> farms came into being, and that men were forced to
> go on the dole and huddle together in dirty slums.
> And it is only since the free rein given to the forces of
> the French Revolution that king after king, in all the
> Catholic countries of Europe, lost their thrones.[4]

Doubtless, this is an idyllic view. Certainly none of us alive today would have enjoyed the black plague. But it must be admitted that we are not as happy, or one tenth as happy as our technology might be expected to make us. The health food fanatics, the conservation zealots, the poverty activists, all have certain points. And in the days when the One, Holy, Catholic, Roman, and Apostolic Church, held sway over the hearts and minds of Europe, when Innocent PP. III, Pontifex Maximus, was truly "Father of Kings and Princes," those points were met, as by-product of the churchly mission of sanctification. Psychologically, western man would never be so well integrated again.

Our own splendid century of the "common man," when the common man has died in greater droves than ever before, will strike the objective observer with its vast difference from, and refinement over, the barbarous 13th. In place of the tutelage evily imposed by a rapacious Church, the world enjoys the benevolent dyarchy of the philanthropic capitalism of the United States, and the democratic socialism of the Soviet Union. Rather than suffer under beighted simpletons like St. Louis IX or St. Ferdinand III, the nations flourish under freely chosen leaders of the Stalin-Mao-Hitler-Mussolini school. We have the supremely effective international arbitration of the United Nations to replace that of Innocent III. Nevertheless, it will be interesting to trace the rise to our present utopia from the chaos of Catholic Europe.

In those days, it was felt that all of Christendom formed an organic whole. The Church provided the spiritual and moral

3,4 Our Glorious Popes, P. 59

direction for all classes. As the pope was the supreme judge, temporal problems such as the abuse of the English by King John were often submitted to his arbitration. The pope called Christians to join crusades against the Moslems who had seized the holy Sepulchre, against the Islamic brethren in Spain, against the Albigenses, who constituted the most severe threat (because of their insidiousness), the Church was to see until our time. Under him, the primates, archbishops, bishops, and priests administered the sacraments, guided laymen, and provided all of what we would call social services (hospitals, schools, orphanages, welfare, agricultural research, etc.)

In the secular world, the apex of power, at least in theory, was the Holy Roman Emperor. He was seen to be first among princes, even if the princes often acted differently than they saw. Crowned by the pope, he was regarded as the successor of Augustus, Constantine, and Charlemagne. Similarly, the kings, crowned by the respective primates of their realms, were supposed to be the primary defenders of the Faith of their countries.

The nobility, feudal rulers under the kings, were in turn defenders of Faith and people, being obligated both to vassals and lords, though in different ways.

The peasantry in the country, and the guildsmen in the towns were the workhorses who kept society supported materially. In turn, they were the ones who benefitted from the charitable activities of the Church, and were most sustained by her in the dark days to come.

Every phase of life was enobled and transformed by the Church. The savage barbarian warriors and decadent Roman Patricians were both transformed into the courtly knights of legend, song, and history. The artisans associations, in lieu of the rapacious unions of today, were guilds, who held the salvation of their members souls, the quality of their products, and the well-being of their bodies above the disposition of their pension funds. Architecture, it must be admitted, was somewhat inferior to ours, producing merely a Chartres cathedral to compete against our stately World Trade Centers. Music called forth the troubadours, trouveres, and meistersingers, to say nothing of chanting monks and nuns. This, of course, did not quite replace Led Zeppelin, but those poor souls did not know what they were missing and did not, we hope, suffer too much on that account. Surely the women executives of our day present a much finer image of equality than the spectacle of a mitred abbess sitting in the House of Lords, presiding over dozens of convents of women and monasteries of men, and held as feudal chatelaine by half a shire? As for the literature of the time, King Arthur, Galahad, Parsifal, Lancelot, Roland, and countless others have remained in the popular mind, inspiring each new generation of writers to embellish and add to their adventures down to the present day. But the point of those tales was very simple; the road to the Holy Grail, the cup of eternal life was kept and guarded by the Fisher King. In that, we have much in common with our ancestors. Peter-in-the-boat still casts his net from Rome, hoping to bring us all to the Grail.

# Prelude to Horror

## The Gallican Crisis

Unfortunately, the golden age was not to last. The benificent forces which have shaped our own paradisical world had not been destroyed by the Church, only checked. Greed, lust for power, ambition, and that old pal of tyrants, rebels, boobs, and everyone else - overweening pride - remained. As in Tolkien's Middle Earth, so on our earth, that it has always been the tendency for the good, the beautiful, and the sublime to be destroyed by the evil, the ugly, and the banal.

As the 13th Century drew to a close, the spirit of the crusades and the concept of the City of God, had begun to be replaced by the desire of secular rulers to determine the moral limits of their rule themselves. Philip the Fair, whose exterior beauty was made up for by his interior disposition, was the first king to open up this phase of anti-ecclesiastical attack.

Philip had his lawyer, Pierre Flotte, forge a false Papal Bull, which purported to represent Pope Boniface VIII's attempt to usurp temporal power in France. Philip demanded satisfaction, closed the French frontiers, and siphoned off monies intended for Rome into his own debt-ridden coffers. The Pope replied by calling a council in Rome despite Philip's ban. A large number of French prelates attended it. Their lands and revenues were sequestered by the king, and somehow managed to find their way into the hands of his creditors. At that council, the Pope, after conferring with Bishops, promulgated the bull, *Unam Sanctam.* This bull reaffirmed the apostolic teaching that the Church was the gateway of salvation, and that no man not subject to the bishop of Rome was a member of the Church. Philip's reaction was not conciliatory. He placed the papal legate under armed guard. Finally, on 13 April 1303, the Pope excommunicated the king.

To say Philip was displeased would not be an overstatement. Not only would excommunication consign the king to hell after death, it would cut him off from the Church and sacraments, and thus release his subjects from obedience to him. How amusing that the same pleasures are available to us today through things like heresy and abortion. Few of us need worry about our subjects today, but at least we can still lose our souls. And through the kind neglect and misinformation received from our up-to-date fathers in God, many of us will be able to experience that ultimate drag! However unconcerned we righteous moderns might be, though, Philip was justifiably disturbed.

Not yet, however, had the Pope officially published the bull of excommunication. If that could be stopped, Philip would not suffer the temporal effects of excommunication. (How modern of him. It would be wonderful to be damned, one supposes, so long as one could still sport a crown, a mitre, or an MBA, without any tell-tale signs of a rotted soul, would it not?) He therefore dispatched troops to Anagni, in the papal states, where Boniface VIII was staying with his Cardinals. As solicitous of their welfare and desires as many of our American bishops are of their own today, they scattered to the four winds. As social workers, civil rights activists, and nuclear disarmament advocates were in short supply, they had to flee disguised as peasants. Oh, your Eminences, Graces, and Excellencies, how true so many of you have remained to one tradition of the Church at least. Whenever the Papacy has been under serious attack, the majority of bishops sided with the enemies of Him who raised them to the mitre. Always was this done in the name of freedom! But we digress, and we have many centuries to survey, and few pages in which to do it.

Two cardinals stayed with the pope, setting an example for brave bishops of our own day. The French troops surrounded the papal palace. Knowing that his death was imminent, he put on his robes, his tiara, his keys, and the ring of the fisherman, which bore the device of the little-fisher-in-the-boat. His attackers did not wish to find the Holy Grail, but to kill the Fisher King. They sneaked through the cathedral, setting it afire, and entered the palace. Impressed, frightened, as Attilla had been by Leo, they nevertheless took the Pope prisoner. Thirty-five days later, he was dead. A year later the Papacy was mired in the "Babylonian Captivity," in Avignon, which we will examine next.

With Boniface VIII, something of truth, of beauty, and of honour went out of Christendom. That this horrible outrage could occur was a clear signal of the route our ancestors had decided upon. Never again would the greatest enemies of the Church come from the outside. No Turk or Tartar could ever again wreak as much havoc as Christians would upon the souls of men. From the day of Philip to that of Fr. Greeley is a long time. But just as John-Paul II incarnates the spirit of the Papacy, so do so many modernist theologians, the bishops who shelter them, and the priests and nuns who murder the souls of children with their heretical poison incarnate the spirit of Philip and, ultimately, of that dark lord who is darker far than he who reigned in Mordor. We may take comfort in the fact that they meant well.

Due to interference from both our old friend, Philip the Fair, and from those distinguished theologians, the Roman mob, the cardinals and the Papacy left Rome for the city of Avignon, in southern France. This was the famous "Babylonian Captivity of the Church," when the popes (all of them French) acted more as domestic chaplains to the king than as popes. The sacred inviolability of the Papacy had received a blow from which it would never recover; during the "Babylonian Captivity" the Papacy's supranational nature began to suffer.

Of course, Rome and Italy were left to the kind attention of whatever robber-baron, brigand chief, or faction, cared to attack them. The faithful began to regard the Pontiff less and less, and to lose their Faith thereby. Truly, the only good thing to have come from that period was the development of Chateauneuf-du-Pape, a superior wine used exclusively at the papal table. It is one of this author's favorites, and he heartily recommends it.

Luckily, after seventy years made bearable only by the wine mentioned, St. Catharine of Siena was able to convince the Pope to return to Rome. Within a short while, however, the Pope was dead.

## The Great Schism

The cardinals elected a new pope, then left for Avignon, where they elected another one, claiming that they had been pressured by the Roman mob. From 1378 to 1417 there were two, and sometimes three popes. The French backed the Avignon Pope, and their enemies the Roman one. It was a dark time filled with uncertainty which grew among the faithful, due to the un-Christian way in which the claimants often acted, the question of which of them was legitimate, and the feeling that God had abandoned the world. The Black Death stalked through the cities and farms of Europe, striking down thirty percent of the populace as a whole, and up to seventy five percent in some districts. It seemed that Satan reigned triumphant over Christendom.

But where sin abounds, where evil seems victorious, so does grace. God raised up men and women like St. Vincent Ferrer and the Brothers of the Common Life; lights that shone in the darkness, though the darkness comprehended them not. In 1417, the Council of Constance ended the schism, and Christendom groaned with relief. Prophetically, the same Council had to condemn Jan Hus. The first chill wind of the Reformation arrived, but a century would pass before the full blow would fall; time enough for rot to set in and pave the way for the great debacle. But all of that must wait for the next section.

During the Great Schism, even bishops were confused as to which Pope to obey. Nevertheless, most did not forget their office. They continued to teach the path to salvation, despite the lack of centralised authority. Heresy did not get the power that one would expect during the rift, and this was due in large part to the courage of the bishops on both sides. They might not have agreed on the identity of the current Pope, but they all knew his powers and the teachings of his predecessors.

Today of course, there is but one formal Pope. But despite that great assistance, the bishops are unable to maintain orthodoxy in America. Indeed, many of them try to destroy it, while the remainder most often allow *experts* to reorder the Faith according to their individual liking. Every priest a pope! At least the Great Schism only had three. Ah, well, let us console ourselves with another Chateauneuf-du-Pape. Wine, at least, retains its loyalty.

## The Renaissance

The century between the condemnation of Jan Hus and that of Martin Luther was one of great promise, great potential, and great failure. The poison sown in the political sphere by the attack on Boniface VIII was imbibed by most of the monarchs of Europe. Great power over the national churches was arrogated by the bishops, who were abetted by their Kings. The intellectual atmosphere was being steadily poisoned by a school of thought called nominalism, which held that most of what are called absolute ideas (dogmas, sacraments, etc.) are in fact mere names. All of these developments, coupled with the rediscovery of pagan literature, contributed toward a more man-centered world-view on the part of the educated, and on the part of a new class, which would leave its indelible mark on history: the bourgeoisie.

To outward appearance, however, things had improved tremendously. Never had the generality of Catholics appeared so pious, never had the Holy See seemed so powerful - powerful enough to revenge itself on both the Empire and France, at least in the military sphere. Michaelangelo, Leonardo Da Vinci, Raphael, and a host of other great artists combined to make the sixteenth century shine.

But mold grows in the darkness, no matter how bright the sun may be. The rising tide of trade created the first of the bourgeoisie - the merchant, banking class. Because they produced nothing of their own they were, many of them, anxious to extend their profits, whatever the cost to church or state. Usury, the lending of money at interest, was forbidden by the Gospels. Christians were thus unable, by Papal fiat, to enjoy that great source of income which had perforce fallen to the Jews, earning them the love of poor artisans and peasants throughout Europe. Such a fabulous trove was kept from the nascent banking class merely by loyalty to the Pope. The Reformation would test for them the love of God against the love of gold. The result is manifest in the present deep spirituality of their mercantile descendants.

Let us now turn to those defenders of the Faith, the kings of Europe. The Emperor, whose oath ran, "I, (N.), Emperor, promise before God and the Apostle St. Peter, that I will protect and defend the Holy Roman Church against all, as far as God gives me strength and power," found his supranational position under attack. His supremacy over all Christian Monarchs had long been theoretical, and its nebulousness was fast being extended to Italy and Germany. Years of struggles with the papacy had weakened the Emperor's reason for being, and not even the assumption by the Habsburgs of the Imperial throne could put Humpty-Dumpty together again. Meanwhile, the kings were busy subduing their feudal nobility, and transforming their crazy-quilt inheritances into modern centralised states. And, while weakening the powers of lords and commons, they cast greedy eyes on all the revenues generated by the monasteries, convents, hospitals, orphanages, and other establishments of the church. They envied the great power wielded by the Church over the hearts and souls of the people. And, as with good old Philip the Fair, they wished to be judged by none but themselves. Against these motives stood only Honour, Loyalty, Devotion, and Piety. We shall measure in the next chapter how well their qualities held the monarchs in check.

Now we may look at the church hierarchy. In Germany, particularly, they were somewhat less than apostolic. The bishops "indulged in excessive luxury, no longer wore ecclesiastical garb, and frequently discarded the law of sacerdotal celibacy."[5] Busy enjoying the revenues of their office, these worthy shepherds were often too busy to look after the spiritual well-being of their flocks. Luckily, they had a large number of expert theologians to do the job instead. Many of these clergy were infected by nominalism, and thus had difficulty believing in themselves, let alone the Faith. The lower parish clergy were often too uneducated to do much more than the recitation of the Mass. Perhaps that was just as well, since so many of the schools were poisoned by heresy. These factors all contributed to making them highly credible defenders of the Church.

The faithful, unlike our present laity, were pious, reverent, and dumb. While devout, and ready to support financially the pressing needs of their fatherly bishops, they were generally ignorant of the doctrine of the Church. They did not demand the favour that their support obligated the bishops to give - true teaching. Thus the seeming fervour of the Protestants, compared to the less-than-edifying behaviour of the bishops, did not repel them by its falseness.

Today, of course, things are much different. Wealthy Catholics stand ready to defend the Faith against all comers. They resolutely take out ads defending the teachings of the Church on abortion, birth control, and euthanasia in all the large newspapers. They teach their children the doctrines of the Church, particularly with regard to financial, marital, and business ethics. They use their financial power to insure that good parochial schools dispense orthodoxy, and that good seminaries turn out well-formed, strong priests.

Don't they? Or are they very much like their predecessors, concerned more for profit? Are they Catholics when it is good for business to be Knights of Columbus, and Masons when it is not? Are they more concerned for their children's MBA's than for their salvation? That the children marry money rather than Catholic? That their views on morality be more pleasing to their friends than to the pope? Surely not!

Although we do not have Kings in this country, we do have

5. Poulet, O.S.B., Dom Charles, *A History of the Catholic Church*, Vol. II, P.3.

politicians. Our Kennedys, Cuomos, and Ferraros always stand tall for the Church. No vote in Congress comes up but they consider Catholic teaching on it. Bravely they insist on the end to abortion, boldly they demand justice for the unborn. They would never consider some mealy-mouthed slogan like "Personally, I am against it, but I would never force my morality on others." These splendid paladins would never stoop to compromise with opponents on Church teaching for political gains, and then trade on being Catholic to get the ethnic vote. The very idea is unfortunately...the case.

Our hierarchy, steeped in the practises of their forebears, contribute their share to the present utopian conditions in the American Church. Our bishops do not neglect their office to act like feudal lords; they neglect it to act like corporate executives. But if the motive behind that neglect differs from their renaissance models, at least the remedy is the same -farm out the spiritual duties to experts! The Faith may die, a whole generation lose their souls, but trips to bishops' conferences can continue, as long as enough faithful keep up the revenues! The experts even have a better heresy than nominalism - modernism! Rather than doubt existence, the modernist may rework the Faith according to his or her own taste - leaving intact the ego expanded so greatly by that effort. The modernists can have conferences, degrees, teaching positions, and parishes. They can murder souls and win awards. Truly the new system is superior to that of the renaissance.

One might suspect that the common faithful would be very different from their forerunners of the pre-Reformation. They would, because they are literate and know the Faith very well. If their children were taught heresies they would teach the kiddies themselves. They would demand the sack of any heterodox priest or nun. If the bishop was lax or slothful in the Faith, they would withhold his funds until he shaped up. If any bishop or priest tried to strip their churches of the beautiful ornaments their fathers sweated, bled and payed for, they courageously would denounce the erring prelates, and demand that their rights as inheritors be respected. If anyone tried to desacralise the Holy Sacrifice of the Mass they would rise as one to defend Our Lord. Or is it just possible that they would sit back and watch their children stolen from the Faith, their clergy turn heretical, their churches be despoiled and the Mass itself debased? No. This is impossible. We have traveled a long road from the 16th century and are wiser than our ancestors. We are very strong. They were not. We shall see the result of this in the next section.

## The Reformation

There is an old saying about "Chickens coming home to roost." It is as true for institutions as it is for men. The Church in the 16th century had enough of those chickens coming home to set up as a rival to Colonel Sanders. Stupidity and laziness always provide their own reward.

It is also a strange fact of human nature that any act, once thought unthinkable, becomes quite thinkable, even pleasant, when at last accomplished. Many forgers, counterfeiters, and child molesters will understand what I mean. Any murderers will catch on too. This is what is called "a bad precedent." Such a precedent had been set by the despoilation of Boniface VIII and the Great Schism.

The last bit of stage setting we must place, is that of the eternal opposition of the spirit of the Church to that of the world; or if you prefer, of Christ to Satan. The Church's keynote in the human sphere has always been intelligent submission to proper authority. That of Satan has been unreasoning rebellion and licentiousness leading to complete slavery. We humans have always prefered short-term gain for long-term loss - damnation on the installment plan. Always an easy plan to sell. And due to the Church's weakness at the time of the last chapter, she was not in a position to restrain this perennial spirit of novelty, pride and power. How could she, when so many of her powerful bishops, theologians and laymen had taken this spirit as their very own? Such a contrast to today!

The history of the Reformation has been too well

documented for us to attempt to re-write it; those interested enough to pursue it can check out our study guide in the back. In the meantime, we can talk about some of the influences on Luther, a little of the action (insofar as it is important to our point) and most of all, the effects, both social and religious.

Luther was a nominalist. This explains the later course of his thinking, much better than his own claim of Roman abuses disenchanting him does. As a nominalist, he could not be sure of the effectiveness of the Church as a means of absolving his sin. As an intelligent man, he realised his own sinfulness; as a man of gigantic physical appetites, he trembled for fear of damnation (perhaps our clergy *could* learn something from him, as the modernists claim!) He could not, due to the nature of nominalism, be assured of the objective value of the sacraments, good works, or anything else. As a priest, he felt this torment to a horrible degree. His main point, then, salvation, by faith alone, relieved the soul of man from any responsibility. Most importantly it relieved the soul of Fr. Martin Luther. It was the most attractive doctrine Satan could ever put before a sinful world - "It's not my fault!"

The kings, princes, and bourgeoisie of northern Europe rallied to the new faith. Not only did Protestantism relieve them of the fear of hell, it took away the last barriers to their acquisition of church property. For the bourgeois, it opened up usury, the primrose path to wealth. Many bishops and priests rallied to the new order, because it freed them of all papal restraint, whether moral or doctrinal. In southern Europe, the kings gave their support to the Pope only in return for greater control over their national churches.

It may be asked, "What of the peasants, the loyal common folk? Didn't they resist?" Indeed they did. In Iceland, Scotland, England, Ireland, Sweden, Denmark, Norway, and Germany, they fought for the old Faith; and they died in droves. Having little effective leadership, as most of the educated opposed them, death was the only result for them to expect. To have defeated the Reformation they would have had to have overcome their kings, lords, and all the weight of the emerging modern state, to say nothing of many of their bishops and priests. Doubtless effective help from Catholic dynasties like the Habsburgs and the Bourbons would have carried the day, but those rulers were too busy fighting each other, the Turks, and the Church itself to bother.

So, the Reformation triumphed. In each country, Catholic or Protestant, absolutism reigned. All the different strata of society that had balanced Royal power were politically destroyed. The Church lost much of its independence to the Catholic rulers, and the State Churches of Protestant lands became wholly-owned subsidiaries of their respective governments. Freed from restraint, the bourgeoisie were able to charge interest on loans, and set the foundation for both capitalism and modern banking. The Protestant nobility had much more property than ever before, and no independent church to tell them how to treat their peasants. The poor no longer had anyone to care for them, but were able to go to cities to starve, rather than enjoy country poverty. Best of all, the religious and philosophical unity of Europe was destroyed. If the Church's authority could be brought down, what else might not be destroyed?

Of course, we moderns, in our ideal position, may wonder what significance the Reformation has for us. The answer is twofold: 1) The forces unleashed in the Reformation are very much alive today. In fact, they have determined the course of our history to the present day. 2) The events preceding and during the Reformation bear an annoying resemblance to the present day. Here is an example:

## BISHOP TO HIS CLERGY

i. That your altars be taken clean away.
ii. Instead thereof you do erect a decent table.
iii. That you set up a table of the Commandments in place of the Sacrament.

iv. That you call upon the people daily
    that they cast away their beads.

v. That you cast away your Mass books
   and all other books of the Latin service.

vi. That you do abolish and put away (out of
    your Church) all monuments of idolatry
    and superstition and all manner of idols
    which be laid up in secret places in your
    church where the Latin service was used,
    and hand bells.    Thomas Bertham,
                       first Protestant Bishop of
                       Lichfield, April 28, 1565 [6]

Despite the fact that Bishop Bertham's orders have been carried out to the letter in most dioceses in America today, the good bishop did not belong to the National Conference of Catholic Bishops. He at least had the decency not to cloak his heresy behind a facade of Catholicity. Would that his spiritual followers of today be as honest. At least we would not have to pay for their nonsense.

## The "Enlightenment"

The last section described some of the more amusing fruits of the Reformation; we must here add one more, perhaps the most important: private judgment. Henceforth, all men were to be free to discern their own vision of reality. How liberating! How refreshing! Open the windows, and let in the draught! That was the great thought of intellectual Europe between 1648 and 1789.

To be sure, a Leibnitz might prove transubstantiation through mathematics; a Bossuet might revise rhetoric in favour of the Faith; a Carvaggio might breath the light of Christ on canvas. But the new philosophers wanted proof! They wanted science! They wanted liberation! The old tyranny of church and monarchy must be overthrown, and replaced with benevolent despots like Voltaire's patrons, Frederick of Prussia, and

6. Crane, S.J. Paul, ed. "Christian Order," Vol. 24, no. 2, p. 124.

Catherine of Russia, both called "The Great."

Luther had granted every man the right to interpret scripture in his own way. Luther objected to any interpretations which differed from his own, of course. The Protestant state churches were unable to generate much fervour on their own, as ecclesiastical appointments became mere civil service slots. Those people who wished to exercise their natural sense of devotion to God retreated in spirit from the sterile religious structures of their lands into irrational devotion. This was the beginning of Pietism and Methodism. Both of these resembled our own American fundamentalism in their denial of reason and exaltation of emotional experience in religion. It was the birth of "that old time religion," complete with revivals and hysteric convulsions.

It may be said in their favour, however, that their hearts were in the right place. They meant well!

At the other end of the spectrum, the theologians and university professors were not idle either. Disgusted with the cynicism of the official Protestant state establishments, and horrified by the excesses of the fervent masses just described, they joined hands with the sillier of the natural scientists. Rejecting the heart completely, they felt that religion should be purely a matter of the brain. They attempted to de-mythologise Christianity by proving that any event mentioned in the Bible which had not happened in the hallowed halls of a university was a pious fraud. They attempted to reduce the teaching of Christ to a tidy little set of maxims. They wished to make the Son of God into a "nice man."

Appealing to man's pride, which always wishes to classify the sublime, and expose the mystery, they inspired the new philosophers, whose doctrines spread quickly throughout Europe. Teaching that original sin was basically a myth, they believed in the essential goodness of man. If man is corrupt, it must be his institutions that make him so. The Church, which had dominated civilised man for over a thousand years, must be particularly to blame. Therefore, it must go! From his height of moral perfection, protected by those two great paragons, Catherine and Frederick, Voltaire could say, "Destroy the infamy." Between orgies, of course. By the latter half of the 18th century the high moral tone demanded by the *philosophes* had debilitated much of the ruling classes of Europe, whose virtue was best personified by Casanova.

While amusing, perhaps, among the nobility, these attitudes assumed horrendous results among that great creation of the reformation, the bourgeoisie.

Before we examine them however, we had better look at their sovereigns. Yet another of the bitter harvests reaped after the reformation is the doctrine miscalled the "divine right of kings." While the coronation formula of "King by the grace of God," had always been held, it was not believed to refer to infallibility.

As long as the king ruled in concert with the church, nobility, guilds, and the other "estates of the realm," he was loyally followed. If, however, he stepped out of the bounds imposed by church and custom, he was likely to be deposed. His authority might come from God, but so did his responsibility. If he misused it, he would pay. The Reformation changed this.

The Protestant kings each became supreme in church as well as state. No longer would an Archbishop of Canterbury call an erring monarch to account; the people must shift for themselves. Thus the adulation received by such a prince knew no bounds. It was inevitable that the Catholic sovereigns would want to cash in on a good deal. Even Louis XIV, however, for all his attempts to rule the Church in France, was restrained by his underlying piety. It remained for the new rationalism to root out that piety from the Catholic kings.

The 18th century produced "enlightened" kings, like Charles III of Spain, Joseph II of Austria, and Leopold of Tuscany, who treated the Church as no more than a method of keeping the people docile. They, or their heirs, would pay for that mistake, for the weakened Church would be unable to prop up their tottering thrones. It is interesting though, that the period opened and closed with three Royal martyrs: Charles I in 1649, Gustavus III in 1791, and Louis XVI, in 1792. All three gave their lives to protect the rights of their peasantry and respective churches from their grasping rationalised bourgeoisie. Perhaps if more of their regal colleagues had followed their example while alive, their deaths would not have occured.

One of the great contributing factors to the spread of rationalism was the fact that the great Protestant powers of Great Britain, the Dutch Republic, and Prussia became much wealthier than their Catholic counterparts of France, Spain, and Austria. The Protestant countries became great banking centres, due to the respectability of usury there. Amsterdam and London became financial capitals. In Protestant realms the enclosures drove many of the peasants off the land, swelling the ranks of the urban poor. These in turn became cheap labour for the burgeoning industries, which were financed by the banks. Since the king was not restricted by custom in the matter of taxation, he could generate much more revenue than could his Catholic rivals. Even if they had better troops and leaders, they would run out of money before he did. Many of them thought that the "Enlightenment's" ideals would allow them to centralise and modernise their countries, so as to compete with the English. Surely it would allow them to hamstring the Church, which opposed their programs. Certainly they had nothing to fear from the mobs of the city, did they?

The nobility, too, degenerated. In Protestant lands, they took advantage of the destruction of the Church to enrich themselves with monastic lands and the tenants thereof. As the capitalist economy developed, and wealth became measurable in terms of cash, tenants became unprofitable. Since the new-born textile industries required a great deal of wool, why not drive the peasants off the land, and replace them with sheep. A spendid idea! And in those places, (like Prussia) where that was not profitable, the ancient liberties of the peasantry were suppressed, that they might be made more lucrative. Most Protestant kings were quite happy to go along with the arrangement; where they were not, they were treated as was Charles I.

Catholic nobles acted a bit better. As most Catholic realms did not develop an industrial base, there was little motive for treating the peasantry as their Protestant brethren did. But under the influence of rationalism, many of them forsook their estates, their duties, and their people, to live at the various royal courts. This did not reinforce their tenant's loyalty toward them, as absentee landlords are hard to revere.

In sum, then, rationalism and Protestantism lead the aristocracy to renounce their ancient feudal role as defenders of the people. The Orders of Knighthood, founded to defend Christendom, too often degenerated into honourary gentlemen's clubs. In fact, anything that savoured in the least of piety or devotion was held to be quaint. The important thing in smart circles was maintaining the proper life-style. Thus when the trouble described in the next chapter hit European society, the noble dandies were often unable to lift their father's swords, let alone use them! How refreshingly different are our elite of today, with their piety, their high moral tone, their concern for the less fortunate, and their valorous defense of American society! Perhaps I exaggerate slightly. Well, at least the movie stars, technocrats, politicians, and jet set of our day have one thing in common with the nobility of the enlightenment. They certainly mean well.

The next group we will look at is the bourgeoisie, who, as the director Louis Bunuel pointed out, have a discreet charm all their own. This was the class par excellence of the Enlightenment. Through banking, new-born industry, and sheer merit (measured, to be sure, in business sense) they had put themselves economically a thousand miles above their humble merchant and artisan ancestors. Those with enough money had themselves ennobled; many managed to live better than most nobles. Singlehandedly they accomplished an economic revolution, which put the world into the shape it bears today.

But monetary success often turns one away from God. I apologize to any pious millionaires reading this book in their private chapels. But generally this is the case. The ability to buy the good things of this world often causes one to revel in them, to the exclusion of God and neighbour. When one is self-made, as were the bourgeoisie, one often tends to credit oneself entirely for success. This of course leads to self-righteousness, pride, and complacency. While we do not mind those qualities in ourselves, they are intolerable in others. Since rationalism made man the centre of the universe, and since the bourgeoisie admitted to being the most able, highest type of man, they were ready marks.

Why should the Church dictate their morals and beliefs? Why should a man sit upon a throne, wear a crown, and rule them, just because his fathers had? Why should the offices of state be almost monopolised by a decadent aristocracy, merely because of inheritance? Why ought one to care about peasants and workers, who showed through their poverty their unworthiness? The old order must go.

The period we are discussing opened with the answer to the problem our heroes were faced with. In England, Charles I, grandson of the martyred Mary, Queen of Scots, insisted on ruling as a king should. As his wife, Henrietta Maria, was Catholic, he favored us, granting our fathers in the Faith tolerance at home, and a refuge in the new world, in Maryland. The independence and Catholicity which he attempted to instill in the Church of England, through Archbishop Laud, was doubtless inspired by the Catholics around him. He protected the peasantry against the enclosures and hampered the growth of England's capitalist system. Under cover of "the rights of Parliament," the extreme Protestants and banking and business establishments, plus those lords who stood to gain from the enclosures, waged civil war against him. Under the Royal banner gathered Catholics, High Anglicans, and peasants. Even today the name of Cavalier conjures up a vision of gallantry, loyalty and honour, traits that have always marked the true Catholic. But industry and profit always triumph over bravery and truth - at least often enough in combat. Those motivated by the most selfish motives are generally better politicians than those not so blessed. The Royal cause was brought down, and money was victorious. It was the first capitalist revolution.

Oliver Cromwell, the new Lord-Protector, was truly a renaissance man. He knew the price of all things, and the value of nothing. In him was the head completely dominant. It was characteristic of him that he outlawed Christmas. It is rumoured that he is the patron saint of bank presidents. However that may be, he certainly was the prototype of the sort of faceless, colourless leader whom all the world enjoys today. It is a pity he died before the computer age arrived.

Under this worthy individual's supervision, all life in merry old England was stripped of colour and beauty. Such things were much too "Romish" for good Puritans. It was an early case, perhaps, of "sanitising for one's protection." Of most importance were the enclosures that continued to destroy England's agricultural class. When the monarchy was restored, Charles II would understand that the bourgeois were in control. James II mistook morality for reality, and lost his throne thereby. Our heroes brought William of Orange over from Holland and began the present system, wherein the British crown is a "Bird in a gilded cage." The remaining Stuarts - James III, "The Old Chevalier," Charles III, "Bonnie Prince Charlie," and Henry IX, "Cardinal York," - tried desperately to regain their throne throughout the period under discussion. Their supporters, the "Jacobites," were a mixed group of Scottish chiefs, Irish earls, English Cavaliers, peasantry, Catholics, and Non-juring Anglicans who were as loyal, devoted, martyred, and romantic as they were unsuccessful. The class of the future was triumphant.

The whole of the struggle between the Church and the Enlightment, which will culminate in the unpleasantness of the next chapter, came to a swifter conclusion in England than anywhere else in Europe. This was undoubtedly due to the subservience of the Established Protestant Church in England. There as elsewhere, the triumph of the Enlightenment and that of the bourgeiosie were synonomous.

Yet another factor which must be considered is that of the New World. This particular area will concern those of us who live here very much. Spanish and Portuguese America, by 1789, had already developed the outlines of the society it would develop down to our own day. It also exhibited the ideological cleaveage between the Church and the Enlightenment that will colour our chapter on Latin America.

North America too developed as a centre of conflict: the Catholic French and Spanish, the genial Dutch and the gallant Southern aristocracy, all played their parts. But the dour Puritans brought Calvin's poison to New England, whence it spread throughout Anglo-American society to transform what became the United States into the bourgeois republic par excellence; by the time of the revolution, interestingly enough, rigid Calvinism had transmuted to Rationalism by the same alchemy at work in the mother country. Once again, however, the reader must wait until the proper chapter to hear any more about it.

Do not suppose, however, that the white hats were doing nothing. The Church, through the Council of Trent, had effected an internal housecleaning which makes an IRS audit pale in comparison. The founding of the Jesuits had spurred both the new missionary movement and the counter-Reformation, spreading the faith to the ends of the Earth and re-establishing it in many places where the Protestants had triumphed. In many Catholic countries, home missionaries like St. Louis de Montfort reinforced the devotion of the peasants - often in the face of opposition from rationalistic, heretical, or stupid bishops. Many charities for the urban poor were founded by devout nobles. Bossuet is only the most famous of a whole galaxy of sound preachers who fought the rising tide of unbelief.

On the political scene, pope after pope attempted to reconcile Bourbon and Habsburg and restore the Stuarts to the British throne to secure Catholic Europe. Unfortunately, those sovereigns, as we have seen, were more concerned with fighting each other and arrogating to themselves as many of the Church's privileges as possible, with little care for the welfare of their common belief. Today, of course, as there are no kings, many of our bishops have taken on themselves the job of frustrating our Holy Father's plans for the Church's progress. Here we see them defending yet another tradition! How edifying! Their Excellencies, Lordships, Graces, and Eminences do mean well!

By 1789, then, rationalism had accomplished the great goal of weakening society through immorality, pride, and division. The next chapter shall show the results. One thing this author can promise: Heads will roll!

# The Horror Unfolds

In my role as a minstrel, it is almost time for me to sing sad songs about the death of kings, to paraphrase Shakespeare. As we noticed earlier, evil things breed in darkness, and by 1788, quite a putrid brood had been produced. The societal decadence described in the last chapter could not continue. If men of all classes had tried to live the life of Christ, the life of the Church, they would have been spared the horror that overtakes them in this chapter. Luckily, our society today is so imbued with the spirit of Catholicism, is such an example of Christianity, that we have nothing to fear in the way of the calamity that seems to stalk and eventually find those cultures which abandon the faith. So let us examine in detail an event too bloody ever to be repeated in this age of Dachau and the Gulag.

When one turns up a rock in the out doors, he often discovers a host of things too pulpy, moist, and disgusting to survive in the light of day. In historical terms, if one turns up the rock of rationalism and free thought, the experience is usually repeated! In this particular case, an interesting rock covered a host of things we must see, to understand what happened to European society. The name we must give to that rock is Freemasonry.

The Freemasons did not originate with Solomon's Temple. Neither did they originate with beings from outer space, or old ladies in Miami Beach, despite the amount of pseudo-mystical pomp with which they are surrounded. The English have always been fond of preserving the form when the substance has gone. They can crown a queen, give her no power, and pretend that they are as well governed by Harold Wilson as by Alfred the Great. They can have the newly-freed barbarians of their dissolved Empire join a private club called the Commonwealth and pretend that they are as great as they were under Victoria. Similarly, many of the guilds survived the Reformation. Powerless, pointless, they reflected (and many still reflect) the peculiarity of the English mind. One of these guilds was that one which had helped, in its days of usefulness and life, to build the English Cathedrals to the glory of God and the Catholic Faith: the Freemasons.

Since by 1717, the Church of England was not in the business of building Cathedrals, the number of Freemasons had dropped off considerably. Therefore, as with any other institution on the verge of dissolution, the craft had to find a new raison d'etre. Since the light of Catholicism had been all but snuffed out in England, and the Calvinistic and Protestant mixture that dominated English religion at that time was none too soul satisfying, a spiritual vacuum had been created. On the continent, the two mystic doctrines of Kabalism and Rosicrucianism were flourishing. Unfortunately, we cannot for reasons of time and space say too much about them here. Let it be known though, that they had a great deal to do with magic, and the direct experience of the divine, and were a thousand times more interesting than the silly cant handed out in the Protestant pulpits of the day. Deprived of the Sacraments, which perfectly provide that which the Kabalists and Rosicrucians seek, informed Englishmen flocked to the study of these two doctrines. The Masonic lodges became possessed of a new purpose: study of occult doctrine, and general good fellowship. The oaths of secrecy formerly maintained to protect trade secrets, were beefed up with magical curses and used to protect the new business of the lodge.

With the love of empty pomp so peculiar to the English, Masonic ceremonial, fed by Hebrew tradition, Islamic ceremonial and good imagination, blossomed into quite a rare flower indeed. In this new and improved form, the craft not only took on new life, but spread onto the continent. In addition to the occult, the study of the new sciences was encouraged.

Rationalism thus flourished alongside magic. Great men of all types, generals, bishops, and even princes of the Blood, joined. By 1788, it was to be found in every civilised nation, and in our own, too.

While most of its members perhaps cared more for camaraderie than Kabalah, certainly the secrecy of the lodges lent itself to the political intrigues with which Europe was rife. Although Freemasonry was perhaps harmless, though rather silly, it was ripe for subversion by a much misunderstood and much talked about group: the Illuminati.

Oh, what visions that word conjures up! What mad theories cluster about its name! Just for mentioning it. I will doubtless lose my loyal readership, who have put up with all of my peculiarities thus far. "To the Moon," will they say, "would we follow you - across the mountains of madness, to far Opar, which died before our world was born, would we go. But to the fabled halls of the Illuminati, to whom every theosophist, Bircher, Tarot reader, and fortune cookie seer claim may be laid every evil in the world? No. There we close the book, dear author, to pick up another Harlequin Romance!"

If this adequately expresses your feelings, dear reader, please bear with me. Let me be not only a minstrel of Gondor, but a stand-in for Rod Sterling on the "Twilight Zone." As Dr. Van Helsing said in *Dracula,* "We must pass through dark waters before we reach the sweet." If we are to understand the nature of that problem, that conflict in which we are engaged, we must examine all factors, freed alike from the strictures of prejudice and the whims of fantasy. And so strengthened perhaps we may turn our attention to the great bugaboo of the "conspiracy school" of history, the Illuminati.

We have already seen the tendencies of the Enlightenment. There must be an end to traditional authority: altar and throne must come crashing down. There must be an end to traditional custom; noble and peasant, artisan and worker must be all alike. Traditional culture too must cease, and with it the death of superstition and the end of all songs. Over this golden age would reign a new order of man; competent, clear-eyed, eminently practical. As long as these were mere ideas bandied about by the less astute, self-proclaimed intelligentsia, they were not dangerous. In the hands of an intelligent organiser, however, one who could take advantage of all the situations described, those same ideas could be the wreck of civilisation.

Adam Weishaupt was such a man. He was a renegade Jesuit with all that order's understanding of human nature; a canon lawyer and university professor, with all the respect attached to that office; a Freemason, with access to that age's greatest avenue of secret continental wide communication, save the Church. As Saruman of Isengard was the greatest wizard of Tolkien's Middle Earth, so Weishaupt too, by education, situation, and good fortune, had the potential to be one of the great men of his time. Had he remained loyal to the memory of St. Ignatius, he could have helped the Church through an evil period in history. But again like Saruman, he was seduced by pride, and by pride's father. He fell.

In the study guide attached to the end of the book, those who wish to learn more in detail can find sources to explore further. Let it suffice here to say that he founded a group with the catchy title of the Illuminati. As punk rock had not been invented, what could a group with such a name do but get into conspiracies? Freemasonry, with its secret oaths, its prominent membership, and its code of blind loyalty to fellow members, provided fertile ground for the Illuminati to spread their ideas and power. By 1788, the ideals mentioned earlier were current throughout the whole of Freemasonry. Men have always been fond of secrets; remember grade school? As we get older, we leave our secret gangs behind us along with the toys and games we played. In our great maturity, we assume the place of grown-ups. But watch us jump to join country clubs, form cliques, and close our neighbourhoods to outsiders. Imagine then, membership in a secret society, with passwords, exotic ceremonies, and impressive costumes! Where we could have titles like "Secret high exalted veiled prophet of the vomitous realm!" We could mingle there with great personages of finance and politics, and claim equality with them. We could contribute money for charity, and be made to feel that we are important parts of the great struggle to create a modern, tolerant, new order for the world. Thus we could be reassured that we do indeed mean well. This was the bait the Illuminati held out through Freemasonry. Their true aims, the establishment of a worldwide slave state based on Plato, with themselves as philosopher-Kings was, of course, too insane for the average man to support. But through the strategems outlined, people who would never have thought of universal revolution were drawn into giving it their support, their fortunes, and their lives. Fantastic? Certainly. Yet, if a certain Colonel Ludendorff, in 1908, had met a shiftless housepainter in Vienna, or an unemployed radical in St. Petersburg, he would have snorted at both of them contemptuously. But he helped both Hitler and Lenin attain power. Thus do mighty toadstools from little sporlets grow.

As is often the way with servants of evil, Weishaupt himself, did not prosper. Having accomplished his goal of infecting masonry, his usefulness came to an end. Bavaria's police imprisoned him and the Church, who had suffered so much from him, reconciled him, and he died. It would be nice if Satan was cheated in the end.

His work lived on, however. The Freemasonic leadership was Illuminist and their ranks swelled. Two of their acquisitions were exceedingly fateful. One was Frederick II of Prussia, called the Great. The other was Phillipe, Duc d'Orleans, cousin to the King of France. One would be the initial financier of the Revolution, the other the instigator. Both would pay, one in the defeat and humiliation of realm and successor, the other through his execution by those he had brought to power.

Then, at last, the ideals of the Illuminati were put into practice. Bloody revolution spread through France, Italy, Germany, and Spain. The monarchs were toppled one after another. Louis XVI and Gustavus III died for their thrones and people, it is true, but all the others fled as occasion forced. Only the Pope was not moved - except by force to France. When it seemed that the revolution would end through lack of leadership, Napoleon arose.

Bourbon of Spain, Bourbon of Naples, Habsburg, and Savoy, all the great Houses of Europe, fell beneath the conqueror. The British held out despite their loss of Hanover, the Ottomans were too remote, and Russia too vast. But all else in Europe owned Bonaparte as ruler.

From the beginning, however, in Brittany, Normandy, Poitou, and the South of France, resistance to the new order flared up. In the Vendee, loyal peasants formed the "Royal Catholic Army." In Spain, in Germany, in the Tyrol under Andreas Hoeffer, the Counter-revolutionaries continued their struggle against Napoleon.

Napoleon himself, as long as he supported the revolution and Illuminism, was successful. But when he was crowned Emperor, when he saw himself as the successor to Charlemagne, when he in fact began to understand the nature of that which had brought him to power, his day of doom was not far off. The financial powers heretofore friendly to him breathed new life into the tattered remnants of the old order, while false counsel drew him into Russia, bane of invaders. His power was broken at the Battle of the Nations at Leipzig, Austria, Russia, Prussia, and Sweden pursued him. Saxony and Bavaria betrayed him, and he was brought to earth. The Hundred Days represented a last roar at unheeding fate by a man whose will was as unconquerable as his end was unavoidable.

At the council of Vienna, the restored monarchs hoped to inaugurate a new era of peace. Through the alliance of France under Louis XVIII, Britain under the Prince-Regent (George III having gone mad,) Austria under Francis II, Prussia under Frederick William III, and Russia under Alexander I, the revolution would be kept down for good.

Unfortunately, this was an illusion. For the monarchs, nobles, armies, and peasants had not been the cause of Napoleon's downfall. They had merely done the work for that confluence of financial and political interests earlier referred to. The bourgeoisie had been won over to the revolution through the experience of power; they would form the nucleus of the old Liberal parties, to agitate peacefully for the things Robespierre murdered for. Para-masonic secret societies flourished everywhere, preying particularly on students and submerged nationalities. For fifteen years, from 1815 to 1830, Church and State enjoyed peace. But then — for that, you must turn to the next chapter!

# The Gilded Age

When the smoke of the revolution had cleared, and all things appeared to have been restored, all Europe groaned with relief. Kings sat again upon their thrones, the Church was freed from persecution by jacobins, and it appeared to all that Humpty-Dumpty had miraculously recovered from his fall. Unfortunately, it was not so.

In 1815, the cleavage was institutionalised. The revolution had truly destroyed the old regime. Louis XVIII sat upon the throne of his fathers, but France was the centralised France of Napoleon, not the collection of local liberties of Louis XVI. The Holy Roman Empire had breathed its last; never again would any claim be made to the crown of Charlemagne, though he who last had worn it was restored to Vienna. Most of all, the economic power of the capitalist bourgeoisie, and the victory of the industrial revolution, were triumphant in all of Europe. The kings and nobles seemed to have regained power, but it was the banking and business interests who had really conquered.

Nevertheless, from 1815 to 1830, this was not apparent. In that time, most of the parties developed that would colour history into our own time.

The first party to consider is the Conservatives. Fearful of the growing class hatred, they felt that the political victory achieved in 1815 could only be safeguarded through a thorough repudiation of the revolution; agriculture must be supreme over finance and industry; guilds must replace exploitative labour; the warring classes give way to the organic state. They required that the Church regain its role as arbiter of morals, and that politics return to the wholesome example of the Middle Ages. We see once again the romantic coalition of nobles, gentry, and peasantry, as brave as they are ineffective, as bold as they are unorganised.

Opposed to the Conservatives were the Liberals. These were the masters of the new wealth; the apostles of the Enlightenment. Armed with the money power, with new ideas (always have we men loved things to be new, regardless of their worth,) and the genius for organisation that those born with calculators for hearts, who see life through a chequebook, naturally possess. They demanded an expanded electorate, so that those lives who depended upon factory work might vote for their employer's choices; an end to hereditary privilege, so that those with more money might rule; indiscriminate free-trade, that farmers might be ruined as a power, and be the more easily bought out. Liberty to plunder, equality for the wealthy, fraternity among thieves. Their wage-slaves were only too eager to believe Liberal promises, especially as the vague Conservative mutterings about love of Soil, Country, Crown, and Cross, spoke little of food or lodging.

The second power to emerge from the ideas of the revolution were the Socialists. They fed the illusions of the proletariat further, promising them not merely freedom, but power. They looked to the overthrow of both the Conservatives and Liberals, both Church and State, and the rise of a new order.

Throughout the nineteenth century, the three groups had radically different attitudes toward the Church. As mentioned, the Conservatives favoured Church privilege. The Liberals wished for separation of Church and State, and the former's confinement to strictly ritual activity; shorn of any practical influence, it would pose little threat to their monopoly of power and wealth. For similar reasons the Socialists desired its absolute destruction.

As the Conservatives would soon be compelled to retreat, leaving the field to the Liberals and Socialists, Catholics would be forced to organise politically themselves, develop their own social theory and continue their divine mission despite the most annoying circumstances.

Having identified our players, we may continue the play. As previously described, the Conservative victory was more cosmetic than real. Owing to the genius of the great Metternich, revolutionary outbreaks in Naples, Spain, Sardinia, Modena, Parma, and the Romagna were put down by the Concert of Powers in 1820-21. In France, Charles X was crowned at Rheims in 1825, with all the pomp of his ancestors, and in 1830 began the conquest of Algeria.

Yet the cracks began quickly to appear. Due to British intransigence, the recovery of Spain's rebellious American possessions was frustrated. In 1830, Charles X was deposed and replaced by Louis-Phillipe, ushering in the "July Monarchy". The great bourgeois became the ruling power, with the motto "Enrich yourself!" Did they ever!

In Spain and Portugal, the defeat of the Miguelists and the Carlists ushered in an era of instability, generally dominated, however, by the Liberals. For the rest of Europe, the writing was on the wall.

Eighteen Forty-Eight and its revolutions, and the German and Italian unifications ushered in a period of anti-clerical and Liberal dominance in most of Europe, while industry grew and the social order achieved the cancerous state it preserves to this day. In the darkness of industrial waste, socialism bred and emerged as a force to be reckoned with while Liberals did their best to destroy the Church's hold over the people; thus did they weaken the best guarantee against socialism and social unrest.

The Church did not stand blithely by and watch herself be despoiled. Blessed with great Popes like Pius IX and Leo XIII, and with bishops like Dunpanloup, Von Ketteler, and Wiseman, the Church organised. Especially notable were the great laymen, like O'Connell, von Windhorst, Goerres, Veuillot, and a host of others. They were ready to challenge all the world if need be for the Faith. Whether flocking to the banner of Pius IX to defend Rome, or building the words of Leo XIII into political platforms to challenge a Bismark or a Clemenceau, their courage did not fail. Among workingmen, in the houses of the wealthy, in parliament, the army, or the university, fine Catholic laymen carried on the struggle of Christ the King, in times of war or peace.

Perhaps typical of the spirit of Church of the nineteenth century was the battle-cry shouted by the Count de Montalambert, which comes to us of the twentieth as both a challenge and a reproach: "Are we (Catholics) to acknowledge ourselves such bastards that we must give up our reason to rationalism, deliver our conscience to the university, our dignity and our freedom into the hands of lawmakers whose hatred for the freedom of the Church is equalled only by their profound ignorance of her right and her doctrines?...We will not be slaves in the midst of a free people. We are the successors of the martyrs, and we do not tremble before the successors of Julian the Apostate. We are the sons of the Crusaders, and we will never retreat before the sons of Voltaire!"

What a slap in the face to us of the twentieth Century's dying years. In the last two decades, our bishops, priests and parents did give up their reason to rationalism, their consciences to the university, their dignity and freedom to such lawmakers as the Count described; they made themselves such bastards as he denounced. We, their offspring, are indeed slaves in the midst of a free people. We successors of the martyrs gladly offer incense to the moral and social gods of those of Julian the Apostate; we sons of the Crusaders believe the superiority of the spawn of Voltaire. At least we mean well.

By the end of the nineteenth century, a certain modus vivendi had been worked out in most of Europe. As Liberal political structures everywhere gained ground, the struggle deserted the blood of the barricades for the rhetoric of Parliament. In most countries, the Liberals would hold office much of the time, while their ideas determined the general political course, whoever was in power. Even in Austria and Germany, where crown, church, army, and aristocracy held power, they were paralysed while banking and business gathered ground. Joviality and philanthrophy masked banking greed.

The Conservatives were mainly concerned with maintaining the dead trappings of a great past. They continued to staff the greater part of the diplomatic and officer corps, and of high society. From being a vibrant power, they ended the century with the position and standing of Christmas tree ornaments.

The Socialists were already displaying the twofold nature that would become a split later on, between those who favoured peaceful revolution and those who loved violence. Slowly, they brought more and more of the proletariat under their sway, and ate away at the foundations of European order.

The Catholic parties had triumphed, in the sense that they had built a place for the institutional Church in the Liberal dominated society. But in their greater task, they failed. Only Catholic social principles could have truly improved the lot of the proletariat and transformed it into a mass of happy Christian labourers, with an integral place in the society which depended so heavily on their work. That failure would doom the fabric of Europe.

It is hard for us who live in the age of the dictators, when horror and atrocity are daily events, and dishonour is good buisness practise, to understand that time. The period of Liberal dominance lasted roughly from 1879 to 1914, and is often called the "Belle Epoque." The rule of money was accompanied by a great growth in material well-being, except for the poor folk who manned the factories. The mix of modern means of production and communication, with quaint survivals from the past, accompanied by the vaguely religious, sentimental optimism Liberals have always exuded, made for a great feeling of well-being in the majority. The spread of education, imperialism, and the sense of forward movement made for a very "Belle Epoque," indeed.

So great was the feeling of well being and reconciliation, that some Catholics felt the time had come to compromise. The Church must be updated to fit liberal tastes. The Church's claim to be the only path of salvation, to unchanging dogma and to divine creation of the world all must be at least re-examined; and probably rejected. St. Pius X resolutely crushed this evil, but could not root it out. At least it was forced underground.

The discontent of the proletariat continued to grow, until in each country the conviction grew among the banking and business leadership that war would get the worker's minds off their problems. They were right.

The catastrophe of the First World War, which ushered in our own period of barbarism and death, was in one sense the product of all the portions of the political spectrum we have described. So let us try to find out who killed the Cock Robin of civilisation.

The conservative kings, noblemen and aristocrats, officers and diplomats who preferred to obey unworthy placeholders, and salved their consciences with the thought of being democratic, betraying the people committed to them thereby; they killed Cock Robin.

The socialist agitators, who wished only to destroy and rule with no thought of the common good, and the foolish proletariat who followed them blindly; they too killed Cock Robin.

The Catholic politicians, who sought only respectability when they sat upon all the real answers to society's ills; they killed Cock Robin as well.

Our Lord allowed the accumulated result of greed, sloth, and stupidity to fall upon the nations. And it did.

A typical example of the part played by the rank and file of European Catholics is described here by our friend, the Count Montalembert. "The Catholics of our day in France have one predominating inclination and one function which belongs especially to them. It is sleep. To sleep well and softly, and to sleep long, and after waking for a moment to sleep again as soon as possible - such has been, up to the present moment, their policy, their philosophy, and, according to some, their greatest gift...When an eloquent voice or a too significant fact has raised around the Catholic Frenchman commotion enough to trouble his peace, he half opens his eyes for a moment and turns a dull, astonished gaze upon the unequal fight which is going on over his head... He yawns and grows impatient of the noise which disturbs him, and finally falls asleep again." Thus is described the quality which, in time, precipitated the first World War.

But in this year of disgrace, 1987, we see a mirror reflection in the Catholics of our own land; despoiled of their doctrine, liturgy, and rights by most of their bishops and clergy, forced to accept abortion, euthanasia, and contraception by their politicians, and told by their own Catholic political leaders that they "must not impose their morality on our pluralistic society". Ah yes, my dear fellow Catholics, let us sleep; let us sleep, and see if we can avoid paying the price our slumber demands. Remember, we young Catholics will inherit what (if anything) is left.

And now dear readers, you are doubtless tiring of all this history. Allow me three more chapters - all will be clear. Your minstrel's voice falters, but there is a bit more of the song to sing.

# Our Own Day:
# Let the Good Times Roll

When the trumpets sounded in 1914, few people in Europe realised the extent of the damage that would be done to the structure of civilisation. The British foreign minister, Sir Edward Grey, shortly after his country's declaration of war, looked out over London from his terrace. As the street lamps were extinguished for the blackout (first of many, this century) he remarked, "The lights are going out all over Europe. They will not be relit in our time." And indeed, they have not been.

The emperors, kings, and noblemen rode off in their spendid uniforms, leading peasants and proles and petit-bourgeois to death or glory in the best Napoleonic fashion. But the new technology of war was as devastating on the battlefield as the money of the financiers was on the domestic front. Austrians, Russians, French, Germans, and the rest bled each other white in four years of truly hellish conflict. Evil Sauron, Lord of the Rings, could not have equaled the horrors inflicted upon Christians by other Christians. It is small surprise that J.R.R. Tolkien was veteran of that war.

In each country, the liberal politicians that had led the masses to war soon tired of the fray. By 1916, most of them would have liked to end it. But neither the lower classes, who had bled for the war, nor the financiers who gained from it, cared to allow that. So figures like Asquith and Bethmann-Hollweg were replaced by more bellicose individuals of the Lloyd-George type. The peace proposals of Pope Benedict XV, which called for an end to the fighting, with mutual restoration of occupied territories, were laughingly rejected by the belligerents, whose governments preferred to wade in blood, rather than to listen to the wisdom of the Holy Father. Only Austria-Hungary under its saintly Emperor Karl I wished to comply, a wish frustrated more by the coldness of the Masonic Clemenceau than by the war-likeness of Kaiser Wilhelm.

Left to themselves, the Europeans would doubtless have ended their "civil war" eventually. Perhaps the exhausted Powers would have been unable to fight another war for a hundred years. In any case, a return to something approaching the status quo ante was possible. Of course, this would not fit the programme of the great bankers and industrialists. Two events occurred, however, which if not initiated by the group mentioned, were certainly assisted by them. They were the Russian revolution and the American intervention. For the future of the Church, Europe, and the world, they were equally disastrous.

Now we must deal with Russia. All of the generalities we have been using applied least to Russia. While St. Petersburg, Moscow, and other cities supported an urban culture, complete with proletariat, over-refined aristocracy, and rising bourgeois, most of the populace was fairly primitive peasantry. While the lot of the peasants was perhaps not as good as that of their French or Austrian conferes, it was better than it is today, most commentary nonwithstanding. (Indeed, under good King Brezhnev, the age-old "Mir" village organisation, which had preserved Russian identity even under the Tartars, began to be dismantled, resulting in disclocation and extremely bad harvests.)

While the established Russian Orthodox Church was slavish to the government, severely anti-Catholic and suspicious of any progress, it was supportive of devotion to Mary. Catholicism, finally freed of restrictions in 1905, worked not only among the Poles, Byelorussians, and Lithuanians of the Empire, but (in its Byzantine rite) also among the Russians themselves. Great converts like Vladimir Soloviev enriched it.

Nicholas II was not the wisest Tsar to grace the Court of St. Petersburg, nor the strongest. But in the natural order he was a good man, and a thousand times better than the petty thugs who have succeeded him to the present. He was in a situation, however, that would have been impossible for many abler men. His realm required peaceful development, but misplaced loyalty to Serbia and the machinations of others brought him a war for which he had neither the strength and discernment to avoid, nor the ability and materiel to fight.

Fanned by outside interests, and fueled by a conflict as destructive as it was apparently unwinnable, discontent spread and in 1917, revolution broke out. The Tsar abdicated, and was replaced by Alexander Kerensky, surely one of the four silliest politicians Twentieth century Europe has produced, (the other three were Franz von Papen, Edouard Benes, and Anthony Eden) who presided over a parliament called the Duma. A Socialist himself, Kerensky could not believe that the Bolsheviks, who formed the militant wing of his party, meant him or Russia any harm. As a good democrat, he knew that the real enemy was the Monarchist Cadet party, and the army officers. He deprived the latter of much of their power over their troops, even while pursuing a new (and totally unsuccessful) offensive against the Germans and Austrians.

Meanwhile, the Central Powers were desperate. It was necessary to get Russia out of the war, if Germany was to be able to defeat the western allies. And Ludendorff and Hindenburg, warlords and virtual rulers of their country, would use anything to win. They found their secret, ultimate weapon against Russia in Switzerland, and shipped it post haste in a sealed train to the Russian front. Its name was Vladimir Ilyich Lenin.

Lenin galvanised the Bolsheviks. In a Coup d'etat, he wrested control from the hapless Kerensky, who fled to America to teach in a university. Whether that is a fitting commentary upon either him or his later career is not for this author to judge, although he has noticed that many university professors (especially Catholic ones) show the same clarity of vision Kerensky exemplified. I suppose that they, like him, meant well.

Lenin held a new election which gave unfavourable results.

Thereupon he dissolved the Duma. But in various parts of the empire military chieftains like Wrangel, Denikin, Kolchak, Yudenich, Bermondt-Avalov, Semenoff and Ungern gathered troops, and began to form the White Army, to oppose the Red one. Lenin's government negotiated the treaty to Brest-Livotsk with the Germans, who occupied even more of Russia. At any rate, Russia was out of the war, and the situation of the Allies was desperate.

Across the Atlantic, though, things were quite nice in the U.S.A. President Woodrow Wilson, who had inaugurated the Federal Reserve Systems, was re-elected in 1916 with the catchy slogan, "He kept us out of War." Of course, there had been little things like the seizure of Vera Cruz and Tampico in Mexico, and in 1916 he would send Pershing there to chase Pancho Villa. But at least he had kept us out of war with any country that could fight back.

It is a matter of historical record that American interests would have been unaffected by the victory of either side in World War I. Neither side would have been in a position to threaten us. As far as sentiment went, while many American WASPS were doubtless in favour of British victory, just as many German and Irish Americans favoured the Central Powers. It would perhaps have been wiser to have followed our traditional practise of leaving Europe alone, and to have confined our attentions to Latin America, whose countries were both closer and weaker. But those who backed Wilson were after bigger game than Guatemalan banana plantations or Brazilian rubber.

In their way, Prussia and the British Empire had served the cause of liberalism and anti-Catholicism quite well in the eighteenth and nineteenth centuries. But in the twentieth they had outlived their usefulness. In the Great War they would attend to each other, but a successor must emerge. And we, lucky folk that we are, were chosen; as, in a sense, were the Russians. By chosen, do I mean that a group of conspirators consciously set us up? Or do I mean that the forces of history so decreed? It does not matter.

Wilson wished to get us into a war most Americans were against. Luckily, the press was, for the most part, pro-British, and propagandised whenever possible. The sinking of the Lusitania gave Wilson a good pretext to flaunt his morality against the evil Germans. Never mind that the Germans had advertised, warning the American public that they would attack British shipping. Never mind that the Lusitania sailed low in the water, and blew up so quickly, because it was loaded with armaments, in clear violation of the Acts of War. Oh, how Wilson agonised! Oh, how the papers shrilled!

When Russia fell to the Reds, Wilson felt that he could join the Allies in good conscience. Now that they were purged of the evil Tsarist regime, they were good democrats! But how does one buffalo a country into war?

Happily, a solution presented itself in the form of a suspected British Foreign Office forgery called the "Zimmerman Telegram," which purported to be an offer on the part of the Germans to Mexico of the Southwestern states, if Mexico would attack the U.S. As if she could! We declared war.

The last German offensive failed in 1918, due to our presence. Wilson's fourteen points were to be the death certificate of the German monarchy, of the Austro-Hungarian Empire, and of millions of people in the ensuing central European chaos and resultant power vacuum. One might say that the Versailles treaty was a veritable "recipe for a holocaust."

In place of the Habsburgs we erected a number of gimcrack successor states, which featured fierce ruling nationalities oppressing their minorities. Czechoslovakia, darling of the democrats, preached freedom and equality - for Czechs. Slovaks, Germans, and Ruthenians fared less well. Yugoslavia and Roumania could boast of similar situations. Even Poland suffered from internal stresses. Oftimes an ethnic Ukranian, Slovak, or Magyar might feel as contented in his own land as a Palestinian in downtown Tel Aviv. This did not augur well for international stability.

Meanwhile, civil war flared down on the Steppe. From 1918

to 1922, Russia was wracked by the conflict of Reds and Whites. Although the Whites were aided to a degree by foreign intervention (American, Japanese, French, British, and others) and by secessionist elements (Poles, Ukranians, Balts, Finns, etc.) the help received was generally more hindrance than it was worth. The second-in-command of the American force in Siberia funneled munitions to the Reds, who profited also with financial aid from U.S. financiers. By 1922, the Soviet Union had triumphed over the Whites.

In other parts of Europe, in Hungary, Slovakia, and Bavaria, the Communists seized power for short periods. In all countries, they broke off from the Socialists, demanding immediate revolution. Italy, with her feeble Liberal government, and Germany, with her forcibly emplaced Weimar Republic, were particularly targeted, Under French aegis, the Little Entente, of Poland, Czechoslovakia, Yugoslavia, and Roumania was formed to provide a "Cordon Sanitaire" against the Soviets, prevent a Habsburg restoration and maintain the treaty of Versailles. Never since the Biblical man built his house on sand had such a skyscraper of cards been erected. But it was the best the Allies could do to preserve the new balance of power caused by American intervention.

Wilson's administration was replaced by Harding's, which promised "a return to normalcy." For the next 21 years this country retired to a truly meaningful round of Prohibition, bootlegging, boom-times, Depression, Charlestoning, flag-pole sitting, and marathon dancing. Leaving the artificial situation we had created for the Europeans to settle, we revved up our collective Stutz-Bearcat, buttoned our Racoon coats, and sped off to the tune of Aimee Semple McPherson and the Hot Gospellers. It was truly the cat's meow.

Holding the bag our European cousins were, as the popular idiom has it, "in a world of hurt." In all countries, the economic picture was bleak. The British Empire was in hock to Wall Street, and multi-national businessmen of the Rothschild-D'Erlanger stripe bought every German property not nailed down. In a day when several billion marks equaled one dollar, a buck went a long way. While our European friends tightened their belts, the politicians in their several parties had no answers.

The Liberals, bereft of their ruling position by the war, split for the most part. Many amalgamated with the moderate socialists. Others aligned with the Conservatives. Classic Liberalism was as fresh and lively as a brand new dodo feather boa, if less useful.

If the Conservatives were numerically strengthened by the Liberal influx, they were ideologically weakened. If they had stood for little except good manners, nostalgia, and genteel poverty before, they stood for less now. Indeed, the new Conservatives had only one programme - to keep the Communists out. Because they were forced to pick up the fallen banner of laissezfaire economics brought in by their new ex-Liberal neophytes, they had to defend the worst excesses of an industrial system which they had not originated and had consistently opposed. In doing so, they were unable to heed the voice of Catholic social teaching. They could not speak to the proles.

The Socialists had been extremely frightened by the Russian and subsequent revolutions. Coupled with an influx of idealistic Liberals, they moderated their programme. They became interested in maintaining order, while slowly implementing Socialism, in order to forestall Communism. Since Socialism is not the answer to man's needs, it was an effort doomed to failure. Nevertheless, it was able to work, in some countries, after a fashion. In its ability to stultify private enterprise, it succeeded in many places in eroding the tax base upon which the payment for the social reforms was predicated. Thus was born Social Democracy.

The Communists went about as lions, seeking whom they might devour.

There was also, in every country, a large amorphous group of disaffected people, patriotic and uninformed, they rejected the Conservatives as conniving pluto-crats. Disadvantaged, oftimes poverty stricken, they rejected as traitors and atheists the Socialists and Communists. Broken peasants, they sought proper remuneration for their harvests. Unemployed workers, they sought their rightful pay and good working conditions. Youth, they were aflame with devotion, searching for ideals. Veterans, they wanted the national honour they had bled for in the Great War. Believers, they wanted Christ to have a place of note in public life. None of the parties offered these things.

Ignored by the victors of the war, excluded from the new League of Nations, the Holy See continued its efforts to remedy the situation. Again, the popes taught the basics of Catholic social theory, so reactionary as to be called medieval by Conservatives, so radical as to be called fearful by socialists. What was this theory? Its foundation was, of course, the Catholic Faith. As the one true Church, she must have certain rights in the state. More than that, she must suffuse the state with her teaching. Education must be in her hands, in order to inculcate each person with the knowledge of the duties each owes to God and neighbour. These duties are perhaps best reflected in the Mass, where Christ the King sacrifices Himself for the lowliest beings in creation. The family is the basis of the state, and the mold of the future citizen. Therefore, the state must protect it by outlawing abortion, contraception, and by guaranteeing a proper wage to the labourer, that he might support his family and acquire property. Private property is the foundation of domestic happiness, and must be as widely distributed as possible. Guilds, unions, and associations must, under the tutelage of the Church, encourage the personal growth of their members. All classes must realise that they are brethren, each of them necessary for the honour of their country, and the glory of God. In short, the popes taught the theory of the corporate state.

The exact form of the state did not matter, so long as it served to maintain the ideas set forth. Many Catholic theorists, however, preferred some sort of monarchy as serving best to make a reality the divine dominance. Heredity would determine the identity of the head of state, even if the head of government was elected. In any case, a strongly hierarchical structure was called for, in imitation of that which holds both in Heaven and in the Church.

Thus originated a whole school of thought, international in scope, which sought to present a credible opposition to both the Socialists and Communists on the one hand, and the liberalised Conservatives on the other.

One idea which united the diverse proponents of this school, or schools, was a fear and distrust of the great international bankers, whom they blamed for the horrors of the World War and the Russian Revolution. They feared both capitalist America and Communist Russia.

Those who favoured the Church's place, and set her at the center of national life, were men like Chesterton and Belloc in England (who called themselves Distributists), Fr. Fahey of Ireland, Fr. Coughlin of the United States, Gomez of Colombia, Maurras, Bernanos, and Maritain of France, and Dom Sturdzo of Italy. Some achieved power, like Dolfuss of Austria, Smetona of Lithuania, and Salazar of Portugal. Some only attained power (unfortunately) under the Germans, like Degrelle of Belgium, Msgr. Tiso of Slovakia, and the Ustashi of Croatia. New life flowed into old organisations, like the Catholic Centre party of Germany. New ones formed, like the Sinarquistas of Mexico, the Action Francaise Canadienne of Quebec, and the Rex of Belgium. It was the day of the Cooperative movement, and the Fishing Parishes of Nova Scotia.

Outside the Church, the same ideas had great appeal. They were adopted by the Iron Guard of Codreanu in Roumania, by the Social Credit of Major Douglas, and by the German National People's Party of Hugenberg. So too arose the Solidarism of the German Strasser brothers and the Russian NTS. But separating the Church from these political theories produced the same result that separating her from the individual soul produces: a monster. The state needs a greater justification for existence than the maintenance of order. If not the sanctification and happiness of man, it must be the exaltation of the dominant race, or of the state itself. Hence, from the same ferment which brought us the wisdom of Christian Democracy, the bravery of a Von-Stauffenberg and the fortitude of a Paul Claudel, also arose Hitler.

The war had trained millions of men in the ways of combat, the joys of camaraderie, and the intoxication of serving a cause. The example of their veteran fathers and elder brothers, and the idealism of the Pan-European Youth Movement, gave the young of the twenties and thirties a yearning, a desire, for an indescribable utopia. In this ground, all of the ideas discussed, Fascist and Corporatist, Nationalist and Internationalist, Catholic and Positivist, mixed, merged, and met. It was indeed the romanticism of the twentieth century. Vague oaths were sworn on mountain tops, huge communal camps were held, ideas were exchanged. It was perhaps inevitable that the veterans and the young should form armed groups: the Camelots du Roi in France, the Freikorps in Germany, and the Arditi in Italy. It was also inevitable that, in pursuing the interests of the state above that of the Church, some should fall into the errors of National Socialism and Fascism. If we, the youth of today, can congratulate ourselves on our superior intelligence, we may also think about our greater indifference. If a hostile government persecuted the Church in America, would we drop all our hopes of career, family, and rush off to the barricades? Would an American counterpart of the Mexican Cristero or the Austrian Heimwehr spring up, vowed to save Catholicism or die in the attempt? Would we be like the brave Knights of Gondor, who rode against Sauron's legions to defend Minas Tirith, despite certain defeat? Prudence and insight often conceal a tepid, weak heart.

It may be said, then, that all the parties we have mentioned were attempts to answer the problem posed by the revolution of 1789; the shattering of societal unity. The liberalised Conservative answer was to placate the masses, while preserving the plunder acquired after the French Revolution. The non-Catholic conservatives (best exemplified by British squires and

Prussian Junkers) wanted merely to be left alone to enjoy their remaining perquisites and status. The Social Democrats wished to end the class struggle by slowly phasing out both poverty and wealth, to create a single class. Communism's answer was to end the class struggle by ending all non-proletarian classes-bloodily; an ideal admirable for its simplicity, if not for its justice. The Catholic Corporatist and Christian Democratic response was to unite all classes in common subjection to Christ the King, although they differed wildly in their methods from each other. Lastly, the Fascists and National Socialists also wanted class unity, but subject to the great god nation, or the great god race.

With the depression, Hitler eventually gained power in Germany. His Liberal-Conservative and Socialist opponents were no match for him; the Communists found in him an equal to their own evil ruthlessness, and the Catholics were like their modern American counterparts, cowed. Many non-Catholic adherents of the Corporatist principles herein described were seduced by Hitler. Would he not restore Germany's glory? Did he not end inflation and unemployment? Did he not put the Jews in their place? (Of course, it was not the Rothschilds or D'Erlangers who suffered, but little Frau Goldberg, or Herr Levi upstairs). The army and the nobility, could not tolerate him, but as long as the majority favoured him, what could they do? As long as the French and British (led by politicians of the same calibre as the resolute Weimar men who opposed Hitler initially) continued to hand him bloodless victories, (like the Rhineland and Austria,) they were powerless. Great democrats that the Anglo-French bureaucrats were, they were able to prevent the restoration of Otto von Habsburg, which alone could have preserved Austria's independence. At least Hitler was elected!

In the ensuing conflict, two great acts were accomplished. First, many Corporatists from non-German countries collaborated with the Germans, seeing them as the only alternative to Soviet or American domination. Thus they were discredited. Secondly, those in Germany like von Stauffenberg or von Moltke were destroyed by the Nazis themselves. Some, as those in Poland, found their deaths at the hands of both the Gestapo and the KGB. As a credible political force, European Catholic Corporatism ceased to exist.

World War II spelled the end of Europe as an independent force. The old Europe, with its different national customs, its relics of Catholicism, its colonial empires, its culture and its learning, was smashed between the mallet of the United States, and the anvil of the Soviet Union. As an example, we quote an extract of Britain's "Catholic Herald," of 6 February 1942: "Two wars are being waged against England. The first we know all about. It is being fought in Europe, in Africa, in Asia. But the second is no less important and no one bothers about it. On this front the outlook is much darker. It is the war against the spirit and traditions of England, and the enemy lies within our gates. Well may German propagandists exclaim that on one side we are being Americanised and on the other Sovietised. Open any paper or pamphlet, and you will look in vain for a mention of "God and My Right," of the ideal of St. George, of the Monarchy, of our constitutional heritage, of our Christian foundations and Faith, of our literature, of our homes that were castles, of our squires, etc., etc., or, if you find them mentioned, it will generally be with an open or veiled sneer." Europe was divided into two zones. The Soviet Zone is run by Communist-native satraps who require Soviet troops to maintain them. The American Zone revived the old Social Democratic-Liberal-Conservative system, with American troops to protect it. The apathy of its citizens would be no match for the Soviets.

The death of Europe presented the Church with innumerable difficulties. In the Soviet Zone, great persecution hampered the Church's work, the collaborators further complicated things. But, the blood of the martyrs is the seed of the Church, and the struggle in Poland produced a man who in 1978 would ascend the throne of Peter - our gloriously reigning Holy Father - John Paul II.

In Western Europe, the Church was unable to halt the victory of the secular state. The example of the U.S. was impossible to resist. Coupled with this was the slow growth of Modernism. Pius X had only driven the movement underground. It grew again after the war, strangling supernatural faith. It spread to America, where we shall shortly see its effects. Finally, at Vatican II, it declared itself openly.

As independent Catholic political thought had been dealt a terrific blow, many Catholics sought an alternative to the manifestly un-Christian economic system prevailing in Western Europe and America. Their faith weakened or destroyed by Modernism, many thought that some marriage of Marxism and Catholicism was the answer. This was the famous "Liberation Theology" of which we will see more in the next chapter. But it appeared that with the end of European political power, Catholics there had lost their own socio-economic voice.

Another effect of the upheaval was the de-colonisation of the third world, which left the Church there in great economic straits. Yet, in his survey of the Church today, Cardinal Ratzinger has said that the Church flourishes today only in Africa, where it is poverty stricken, and in Eastern Europe, where it is openly persecuted.

For the first time since the days of Constantine, the Church is without a temporal protector. Her lay folk echo the political maxims of their anti-Catholic neighbours, and often their spiritual ones. Europe has adopted the ideals of 1789, whether in capitalist or communist form, and the world is divided between the U.S.A. and the U.S.S.R. Europeans have formed the Common Market, and a European Parliament sits in Strasbourg. But if they would have a real union, and not be a mere imitation America, they must embrace the Faith and social principles of the Church that crowned Charlemagne. If such a thing came to pass, then the greatness of the Holy Empire would return. As Otto von Habsburg has said, "The Cross does not need Europe, Europe needs the Cross."

In the next two chapters we shall tell the story of Church and State in Latin America and our own country. You who have waded with me, fear not. The story of the fair and sorrowful damsel Ecclesia will shortly be finished. And then my friends, we shall speak of freeing her from the enemies who enslave her, and of aiding her champion, the proud Polish captain in the City of Seven Hills.

# South of the Border, Down Mexico Way
## or
# Our Buddy, Juan Peron

Let's Mambo! But before we do, let's have a burrito at Taco Bell! That is to say, my friends, that we are going to examine the land of Carmen Miranda, Dr. Mengele, "The Boys from Brazil," and Bomba the Jungle Boy. We are going to enjoy tangoing through Latin American history, in order to prepare for our look at ourselves in the next chapter. So, let us pour out a margarita, ready some salsa and doritos, and plough in.

It may be that some of our readers have been to San Juan Capistrano, the old mission where the swallows convene to watch the flocks of humans that mysteriously gather there each St. Joseph's Day, for no reason apparent to even the wisest swallow. Or perhaps some have been to Taos, New Mexico, to get in touch with their inner karmas. Mayhap they have Mardi-grased in New Orleans or Mobile, been forced into a Chicano studies class in a Liberal-Socialist university, or just defrosted a "Banquet" refried bean dinner. Whatever the case, it will be apparent that Latin America does not end abruptly at the U.S. Customs Station in San Ysidro, but rather peters out somewhere between the Wine Country of California, and that famous "Rose in Spanish Harlem." In actuality, large portions of this country are as much a part of Latin America as Buenos Aires or Patagonia; even more so, because in large parts of Buenos Aires - Spanish is replaced by the gabble of Russian, German, and English. The non-Welsh speaker will be stared at in Rawson, Patagonia. There is even a town on the Amazon in Brazil where the descendants of defeated American secessionists treasure a Confederate flag, sing "Dixie," and drawl out "The South shall rise again."

Latin America is as diverse as Europe or the United States. But, as with both those areas, there are certain social, religious, and political traits common to the whole region. Since the present unpleasantness in Central America, our national attention has been focused in its usual Helen Kellerish manner on the southern brethren. It is unfortunate that the American populace has only realised recently that Los Angeles is closer to El Salvador than it is to New York.

The most arresting difference between us is the fact of colonisation. The United States was initially settled by the English Puritans, who came here to ensure that none of their membership would have the opportunity to enjoy himself. Like their co-religionist Oliver Cromwell, they outlawed Christmas, and even today the phrase "Banned in Boston" conjures up visions of baboonish ignoramuses outlawing Shakespeare because of the Bard's profanity. The more nauseating of their cultural traits were abandoned. Unfortunately, their shortsighted love of profit, their suspicion of emotion, their speed in abandoning honour for material advantage have become seemingly indelible traits in our national character. Only massive immigration has partially diluted the "demon seed."

Luckily for their mental health, piety, and geniality, Latin America was first colonised by the Catholic nations of France, Spain, and Portugal. While the defects in those countries' political natures made the course of Latin America's civil life rather rocky, their Catholicism ensured that more of their subjects would attain Heaven than in the Great Colossus of the north, whose great wealth, stable politics, and indifferent tolerance often provided a hotter fate for its citizens.

Another great difference between north and south is the racial makeup of their inhabitants. Since conditions in Great Britain were much worse than in France, Spain, or Portugal, it was always easy to find settlers for the thirteen colonies. But as neither unenclosed farmers, prosperous bourgeois or great lords showed any disposition to leave the happy life of the Catholic monarchies, it was not easy to recruit colonists there. Those who did come were generally the most turbulent elements in society: lesser nobility, seeking the life of great lords; demobilised soldiers searchng for glory; outlaws yearning for wealth and respectability. Just the sort to conquer an empire; hardly the type to maintain a prosperous, stable nation.

Their pure-blood white descendants came to be called criollos, or creoles. They developed a unique culture all their own. Wealthy with the proceeds from great estates granted by the king, they cultivated an aristocratic attitude that outdid even the grandees and grand seigneurs of the mother countries. With an ethos of honour that made each insult a life or death affair, an education that introduced the ideas of the Enlightenment even while it maintained the attitudes of feudal nobility, and a disposition that denigrated labour and finance, they made the finest of friends and the worst of managers.

Their mixed blood cousins and descendants, generally the result of the shortage of European women, were called Mestizos. They occupied a subordinate position in society, and were generally shopkeepers, artisans, peasants: in a word, they were the work force.

The Indians, preserved by the Church from the unpleasant fate suffered by their northern brethren at the hands of the English and Americans, formed the unskilled labour. Peasants and miners, they had suffered greatly at the time of the conquest. But quickly converted to Catholicism, they would soon enjoy a life both spiritually and materially luxurious, in comparison to that of their pre-Columbian ancestors.

The blacks were brought in as slaves. But unlike those unfortunate enough to be taken by the English, the Latin Blacks enjoyed the protection of the Church, so well exemplified by St. Peter Claver, "The Apostle of the Slave Trade." Their families could not be broken up as could and were those up here in El Norte. Children fathered by white men upon black women had to be acknowledged and reared accordingly. If the man were unmarried, he must marry his slave after freeing her. Thus arose that class called in New Orleans, "gens de coleur," gentlemen of colour. At the same time that half-breed slaves brought their good Protestant fathers greater profits in the States, mulatto Latins inherited slaves and plantations of their own. Ah, the superior Anglo-Saxon civilisation!

The administration of the colonies was entirely in the hands of European-born subjects. Creoles were excluded entirely. This had the beneficial effect of insuring unity of command, and discouraging undue independence of colonial officials. It had the unfortunate effect of depriving the Creoles of any experience of exercising authority, while encouraging their thirst for it.

The Church, however, was open to all. In the seventeenth century there appeared five saints in Lima, Peru. SS. Martin de Porres, Turibius, Rose of Lima, Francisco Solano and Juan Macias represented a true cross-section of colonial Society. The Church protected the Indians and blacks, provided all education and social service, and maintained peace among classes. Her missions in Paraguay, Florida, California and New Mexico helped to create a productive hybrid culture that only guns could silence. As her work in the Americas had been inaugurated by the miracle of Guadalupe, so her growth was miraculous.

On the balance, and for the majority, colonial life in Latin America was probably more humane, healthy and sane, than that in the thirteen Colonies. The very characteristics which prevented the descendants of the Spanish, French, and Portugese from conquering those of the English also saved them from becoming a nation of neurotics, as did the Anglo-Saxons.

This ethnic stratification has in general persisted until the present. In Argentina, the majority of the Indians were wiped out after independence, in campaigns patterned after our own against the Plains Indians. In the other countries, the exact proportion of the different racial groups varies, and post-colonial immigration has altered the situation somewhat. In Sao Paulo, sushi bars are as popular as on our own beloved Sunset Strip. But just as the customs and beliefs of the Pilgrim daddies are still held in reverence as quintessential Americana (even though they are not actually practised outside the Brahmin reservations in

Boston's Back Bay and Beacon Hill, and in strange New England backwaters where one's wife is often one's sister), so to a great degree the Colonial ethos still prevails in the lands of Chili peppers and the Conga.

Our readers will remember Napoleon sweeping over Europe. Two of the countries he swept over were Spain and Portugal. The Portuguese royal family fled to Brazil, and set up regal shop in Rio. The Bourbons of Spain were not so lucky, and were forced to enjoy the hospitality of the Emperor of the French. For roughly fourteen years savage conflict enveloped Spain as the puppet government of Napoleon's brother, King Joseph, fought the Cortes of Seville, still nominally subject to the imprisoned Ferdinand VII. While opposed to the French, the Cortes was in favour of the ideals of the Revolution, particularly the anti-clerical and anti-absolutist ones. When the French were finally defeated in 1815, the Cortes was in firm control of the country. Upon his return to Spain, Ferdinand agreed to the Constitution imposed by Parliament, but at the first opportunity he restored both the Church's rights, and his own. Revolution broke out, and with the help of both his loyal subjects and another French army sent by his cousin, Louis XVIII, he had restored normalcy by 1821.

Meanwhile, Latin America had problems. During the war in Spain, colonial officials loyal to King Ferdinand, King Joseph, or the Cortes squabbled among themselves. With a lack of direction from the mother country, threatened by British, Indian, and piratical dangers, and thrown upon their own economic resources, the Criollos quietly assumed power. Many of them held the ideas of the Enlightenment, and were intoxicated by the North American republic. At first cloaking themselves under loyalty to the powerless Ferdinand, they were forced to declare themselves after Waterloo. Bolivar in the north, and Miranda in the south, had defeated the native Loyalists by 1825. Mexico, strangely enough, became independent through the action of the Spanish Commander-in-Chief, Agustin Iturbide. Fearful of the victory of the Cortes, he declared Mexico an independent

Empire in order to safeguard the Church and state from the evils of Liberalism, Masonry, and the revolution. Being unable to procure a Bourbon prince to assume the Crown, he became Emperor Agustin I. He proclaimed tolerance for all beliefs, political and religious; the next year he was deposed by the Liberals. At any rate, by 1826 the last Spanish troops had left the mainland of Latin America; Brazil had become an independent empire under the son of the Portuguese king. The British prevented, through their control of the sea, any action to reconquer the errant colonies. For better or worse, independence had latched onto the South and Central American nations.

From the beginning of the national era, two different parties emerged in Latin America which dominated Latin politics to the present century. In addition, two other phenomena emerged, which complicated the situation further. We shall examine both aspects.

The first phenomenon is that of "Caudillismo." The Creoles, used to running great estates, deprived of any experience in governing, tended to act, when in power, more like medieval barons freed from royal authority than like public servants. Often politics were more private feuds than anything else. Thus much of Latin public life had all the stability of prize fight. personality overcame principle, and patriotism was at a premium. Few indeed in politics were able to rise above the struggle, and emerge as statesmen.

The second phenomenon is militarism. Due to the extreme polarisation of Latin society, only the army stood out as a national force above party. hence the continuing cycle of ineffective civilian governments, paralysed by dissension, being replaced by "reform" military regimes. Thus coups-de-etat succeeded each other in dreary repetition to our time.

The first party we must consider are the bad guys; those who were called Liberals. They were the children of the revolution, of the Enlightenment. Like their European counterparts, they wanted several things: they wanted liberty: the liberty to abolish the feudal obligations they held to their peasants so as to enslave them like factory workers in Leeds or New York; they wanted equality: the equality of plunder from the church, and from the haciendas of their Conservative rivals; they wanted fraternity: that fraternity described by the phrase, "thick as thieves." From these basic principles came their party programme. They wished to nationalise all Church property, sell it and keep the profits; to separate Church from State, and school from Church, as the Soviet Constitution so aptly describes it; to remove the Church's influence from national life, so to leave the lower classes at their mercy. They favoured decentralised government, since smaller provinces were easier to rule as private property than were large nations. In truth, for all their talk of modern progress, they were no more modern than the pirates who plundered the Spanish Main. They were not even as honest about it.

The other Criollo faction was the Conservatives. Many of these had favoured continued, if looser, links with Spain to offset the lack of centralised native authority. With the total defeat of Spain and Portugal, they looked to establish native monarchies. Except in Brazil (whose emperor was finally deposed in 1889 by the Liberals for the unforgivable crime of freeing the slaves) they were unsuccessful at this too. Finally, they settled for strong central governments, and safeguarding the rights of the Church and the peasantry.

The conflict between the two was unequal from the start, as the Conservatives wished to save a humane system, and the Liberals wished to impose one which was new and different, though barbarous. The Liberals controlled the media, and had the assistance of that great bastion of old Liberalism, the United States of America. Out of hatred for Catholicism, the colossus of the north would gladly arm a Juarez against a Maximilian, or support a Somoza. In return, when in power, the Liberals gladly gave American companies control over natural resources. Little by little, as the 19th Century wore on, the Liberals came to predominate in most of Latin America. But there was one light, at least, to brighten the Liberal gloom - Garcia Moreno.

Gabriel Garcia Moreno ruled Ecuador in the 1860's, and

early 70's. Catholic and Conservative to the marrow, he freed the Church entirely from state control, even while expanding state support for her. He consecrated the country to the Sacred Heart, and ruled as the ideal Conservative. Of course, there was a great deal of progress in the way of education, highways, nutrition, economic growth, and the salaries of the poor. Moreno proved that if the soul were fed, the body would soon follow. His rule showed that the spiritual and economic desert the Liberals advocated was not the only alternative. Needless to say, his administration was fiercely opposed by the American ambassador, who applauded his assassination.

Industry eventually came to a few of the countries of the region. Owned by foreigners, it did little to benefit the host countries, except to create a class of poor, discontented urban proletarians. If the relatively stable European society could not integrate the proletariat, it can be imagined what would result in Latin America. Liberal predominance resulted in agricultural chaos, so thousands of peasants fled the poverty of the countryside, to relaxing urban squalour. Thus was provided a fruitful green space for Socialism, when it made its way to our southern neighbours.

Another factor which would aid the growth of communism was anti-Americanism. Although the power of the Church and the Conservatives had been destroyed, the lingering resentment against the U.S. spread to many places in society. When allies presented themselves against "Yanqui Imperialismo," the Latins were very sympathetic to their causes. Hence the inter-war period saw both native and foreign fascist and authoritarian movements flourish. Not only did they present an answer to the problems of a fragmented society, their very existence thumbed noses at the "arsenal of democracy." This was heady stuff for a proud people, forced to accept the economic mastery of a nation they considered culturally inferior. After World War II, the greatest challenge to the U.S. came from the U.S.S.R. Even a Liberal can figure out the most obvious (if spurious) conclusion.

Churchmen, too, were faced with the humiliation of having

to "co-exist" with U.S. backed Liberal governments, whose anti-clerical attitudes were equalled only by their typical Liberal injustice toward the poor. To survive, they must be silent. The only solutions were to either (a) slowly convert the Liberal oligarchy, while building up the Faith of the peasant to prevent class warfare and to peacefully redeem the situation, or (b) to rally the remnants of the Conservatives, and attempt to replace the Liberals. The latter was the desire of groups like the TFP, about whom you can find out more by checking the organisation guide in the back of this book. Both of these solutions would take time, however. As long as churchmen realised that their primary mission was to save souls, this was not a problem. Unfortunately, the spread of Modernism destroyed the supernatural belief of many clerics and made them forget their role as agents of salvation. If, then, they are not to provide the sole method of entry to Heaven, they must bring about the kingdom on Earth. But the solutions mentioned were incapable of bringing about the kind of immediate change that these clergymen wanted. Who could? Who had the utopian ideals, the zeal, the weapons and support, the ruthlessness, to destroy the present unjust order, and replace it with the utopian kingdom of God? Only the Communists. From the unholy alliance of Church and Reds was born Liberation Theology, which emerged to capture the hearts of Modernists all over the world, and to transform Catholic organisations, even in our own land of the free, into instruments of Communist subversion.

Once again the old dilemna of capitalist versus Communist ensnares Catholics and makes them slaves of the one, or toadies of the other. Once again, we betray Christ and His Church to put them in the service of some political force instead of our own. Today the Communists rule Nicaragua and are attempting to take over El Salvador. We up here in El Norte must take steps to destroy this menace, the ground for which we prepared. If we do not, we shall learn at first hand just how close El Salvador and Los Angeles really are.

Merely defeating the Sandinistas, and even freeing Cuba,

however, while solving our immediate problem, would not solve the Latin conundrum. Only the victory of Catholicism, and of her social principles will do that. As Garcia Moreno demonstrated, the Kingship of Christ will make our Southern neighbours truly liberated, truly free, truly fraternal. Unless the Church triumphs there, we will find our downfall at Hispanic hands one day. Unless the Church triumphs here, we will deserve it.

Our president's battle against the Sandinistas, and our pope's battle against the Modernists and Liberation Theologians are the only things that will save our bodies and souls, respectively. If we do not do our part in both, we have only ourselves to blame in losing a noble people, who by rights are our natural allies.

In our inimitible American style, though, it is more probable that we will just continue to drink our margaritas, indulge our lusts and fry our minds until judgement day. In any case, our next chapter will close our ballad of the past with the story of our own country. I will drink another pina collada, tune my harp, and finish my song.

# Bye, Bye Miss American Pie
## or
# Why We Live In the Land of Oz

Now, friends, your minstrel must sing his last ballad. Not, alas, of knights, dragons, damsels, and wizards, but of hot dogs, baseball, apple pie, and Chevrolet. The land of "Ozzie and Harriet," "Leave it to Beaver," and "Deep Throat." If we are ever to understand the contradictory nature of Catholicism in America, we must understand the nature of America, where half or more of the nation is upset by the visit of President Reagan to a cemetery where half-a-dozen S.S. men rest in well deserved obscurity, but care nothing for the millions of infants slain (and then used for industrial purposes) every year in our own country; where the evils of South Africa are regularly condemned, but the system of death camps in the Soviet Gulag (which would have pleased even the pickiest Gauleiter by their efficiency) which dwarfs anything the Nazi's did, are ignored. In short, we must explore the condition of our own minds.

"In America there has always been a market for a certain kind of cheap thought. It came with the inheritance bequeathed us from Northern European Protestantism, the Protestantism of the dissenting churches that idealised individual effort, believing in man's infinite capacity for self improvement. Cheap thought glows through the work of Henry David Thoreau, who loitered around Walden Pond recording spasmodic thoughts that were as likely the product of his ague as his intelligence. He produced vast quantities of cheap thought for Americans of the Liberal persuasion, but the capitalists too have had their oracles. The go-to-it philosophising of Dale Carnegie is cheap thought and nothing more." Thus speaks R. Emmet Tyrrell, Jr., in his marvellous work *The Liberal Crack-up,* on p. 132.

This mad optimism is perhaps the most unifying point in American thought. Our "Conservatives" often believe that all would be well if only we would return to that great idol, "The ideas of the founding fathers," allowed big business to perform its role unfettered by government, and relaxed while the resultant technology made the U.S. a veritable heaven-on-earth. Our "liberals" believe that all would be well if we made reparation for all the atrocities we have committed to blacks, Indians, Hispanics, Orientals, women, gays, whales, seals, lab animals, indeed, everyone but fetuses. If we then abolished private industry, went back to the land, and lived in a sort of neverending Bambi cartoon, we would have the kingdom of God on earth. Two sides of the same counterfeit coin.

More than any nation on Earth, we search for sublimity in fads. We have an aching need for meaning, for truth, for beauty, and we try to satisfy it with mood rings, pet rocks, and pornography. When we cannot find the Holy Grail in pleasures and fads, we give the "old time religion" a whirl. Thus, as we will see, American socio-religious history is a history of pendulum swings, between an unnatural puritanism, and an unnatural pursuit of pleasure. The roots of this lie in our history, and in the totally un-Catholic nature of our culture.

In the beginning was Plymouth Rock and the Pilgrim Fathers, whom we met in the last chapter. Armed with the ardour of their hypocritical faith, they did their best to wipe out all traces of the old pre-Reformation English merriment that they could. Those familiar with Nathaniel Hawthorne's story, "The Maypole of Merrymount," will recall what treatment was meted out to those who possessed even a fraction of the old Catholic joy. God showered material riches upon those who were saved, so that wealth became a sign of salvation. The poor deserved their fate. And, as the great H.P. Lovecraft observed, "In attempting to follow an inhuman moral code, the early Puritans became adept at hiding things. In time, they lost all taste with regard to what they hid." Attempting to follow even a moderate morality, with all the graces the sacraments afford can be difficult. Without those graces, and with the twisted morality of Calvin to obey, one can imagine the hypocrisy and despair which characterised the descendants of the Puritans. Thus was developed both the ideal of limitless self-improvement and limitless guilt.

From this neurotic ferment, however, arose a discontent which drove the American to conquer the plains, to excel in industry, to be a hard charger, to have ulcers, and to feel guilty. Since most native American religion had a Calvinistic base, it was easy for Puritanism to become the ethic, if not the creed, of virtually every inhabitant of our glorious Republic. Those not so blessed were generally put out of the way.

While Puritanism dominated New England, a more laissez faire Anglicanism dominated the South. Under the British king, however, those landed gentry in New England were also Anglican. The small merchants, tradesmen, and bourgeoisie tended to control affairs in the North. In New York and the South, however, a much more Aristocratic society evolved. Spurred by the slave trade, a society somewhat akin to that of Latin America, without the benefit of Catholicism, developed.

Where did the Catholics fit in? They didn't. Except for Maryland and Pennsylvania, where she was protected by royal fiat, the Church was outlawed by the self-governing colonists, and the crime of being one of her priests was punishable by death. Hence the Protestant night was almost complete.

In both New England and the South the state churches decayed in the same manner as in Protestant Europe. The ideas of the Enlightenment captured most of the educated. Despite the Great Awakening of the 1720's (the first of our periodic religious frenzies) by the last half of the 18th century, American religion was at a low ebb, for all the established churches. Men like Franklin, Jefferson, and Sam Adams, while being great trendsetters before the revolution, were devoid of the most basic faith in Christ.

Before 1763, the French and Indians kept the American colonist hemmed in east of the Appalachians. Due to the nature of their culture, which was founded in opposition to the Royal Authority, the Americans were unable to mount even an effective defense against their enemies because of a refusal to organise. Had the British King not sent over new armies every year in wartime, the Colonists would have been swept into the sea.

With only an eighth of their opponent's population, the French in America fought the American colonists for 150 years. With little aid from France they were able to deal with the regular British army, to say nothing of the colonial militia. But in the end, they were defeated.

With the fall of the French empire in America, the British crown was faced with three dilemnas. First, the debts accruing from the war must be paid. Secondly, defense of the colonists, whose showing in the war seemed to prove their inability to protect themselves, must be continued. Lastly, the rights of the new French and Indian subjects must be provided for. It was the attempt to remedy these problems that would provide those who favoured dissolution of the ties to the crown with their pretexts.

Due to the protection afforded by the crown from their fellow-colonists, most Catholics were loyalists during the revolution. But the services rendered by individual Catholics like Charles Carroll of Carrollton (who signed the Declaration of Independence) the raising of two regiments of Catholics (called Congress' Own) and perhaps most of all, the decisive intervention of France and Spain in the war secured the legal emancipation of the faith afterwards.

However, the Church faced intense prejudice, due to its allegiance to a "foreign potentate," the Pope. Nevertheless, in the period preceding the Civil War the Church made a few notable converts, although not anywhere near the number that were made by the new religions, such as the Mormons, Adventists, and Disciples of Christ. This was perhaps brought about by a fear that extensive evangelising would bring the fury of the mob upon the Church, as happened in a small way with the deservedly named "Know-Nothings." Doubtless the Apostles would have sympathised with this fear of unpopularity.

Nevertheless, expansion occurred on a large scale, before, during and after the Civil War. Annexation of Louisiana, Texas, California, and the Southwest brought many Spanish, French, and Indian Catholics into the U.S. Immigration on a vast scale from Ireland, Poland, Italy, French-Canada, Austria, and Germany both altered the ethnic complexion of the country, and swelled the size of the Church.

Since the Irish were the only English-speaking group in the lot, it was perhaps natural that Irishmen should monopolise the places of power in the American Church. Unfortunately, they brought with them a sneaking admiration for their former English Protestant overlords. This "coachman's complex" made them only too willing to compromise with the Protestant establishment in America.

There were, then, two crypto-factions in the American Church: the mass of the faithful, concerned for the most part with making a living and practising their Faith among themselves; and the hierarchy, who took advantage of the unquestioning loyalty of their people to become a political power. It was the ideal of the bishops that the Church in America must become truly "American." The bizarre customs of the Slovaks, Croats, and Ruthenes must be assimilated as quickly as possible, and the old tongues must be entirely replaced. So-called "National" parishes were to be tolerated for as short a time as humanly possible. The Church's claim to be "the one true Church, outside of which neither salvation nor holiness can be found," must be quietly ignored. The intolerance that Truth reserves for error must be replaced by interfaith equality and understanding. No large scale conversions must be made for fear of upsetting the separated brethren. All authority must appear democratic, no matter how arbitrary it might become. Though there were exceptions like Corrigan and McQuaid in the 19th, and Hayes and McIntyre in the 20th centuries who differed, bishops of the Gibbons-Ireland School prevailed. Thus was incense offered to the gods of the state, thus was gold offered for Christ. The reward sought in this case was recognition and respectability.

The effect on the laity was to make them unconcerned with the spread of the Faith. The bishops would run things, the priests would minister the sacraments, the nuns would teach the children. Layfolk need only "pay, pray, and obey." Slowly, imperceptibly, the Church became more a cultural phenomenon than the True Faith which Christ commanded to be spread, at least in the minds of the faithful. The two World Wars accentuated this trend, for the beliefs of friends made in wartime often seem legitimised. In addition, the ghettos of the immigrants began to break down. With them slid the Faith.

By 1962 the bishops had attained political success, and a Catholic president sat upon the American throne. Never mind that Liberalism and Modernism had rotted the minds of large numbers of the brightest and the best of America's priesthood. Never mind that the Faith had become mere rote for many of faithful. What should their lordships care? Were there not revenues pouring in?

Meanwhile, mainstream American culture had followed its predictable course. The steady decay of religion, and corresponding outre' behaviour was punctuated by even more bizarre attempts at moral regeneration (the most spectacular, silly, and annoying of which was prohibition.) Protestant Liberals traded God for man, and cooked up the social gospel. The fundamentalist faction, on the other hand, followed their spiritual ancestors of the Great Awakening and the Great Revival of the 1840's by reaching back into the worst excesses of the Puritans. Bit by bit, the general moral tone of American life became more hypocritical, more divorced from reason. The schizoid chickens were ready to come home to roost.

The stresses of the bomb, of being the worlds greatest power, of the dehumanising technological revolution, and of mainstream Protestantism's hold on national culture propelled our society toward a real upset. With the end of the 1950's, non-Catholic America was also poised for cultural upheaval.

The age of Camelot was (to date) the last spat of our

American utopianism. John F. Kennedy seemed to hold the path to the future. There were civil rights marches, war on poverty, the space programme. There was folk music... Peter, Paul and Mary, Joan Baez, and Judy Collins. It was at that time that Professor Tolkien's books became popular. Jackie was lovely, and it appeared that everyone would be free, happy, slim, and close to God. We would change the world. Then JFK died, and the party fizzled.

His successor, LBJ, promised that his reign would continue his former employer's policies. He did so and he carried it even to a place called Viet-Nam.

Of Johnson's dishonourable campaign against Barry Goldwater, his gaffe with DeGaulle, and sundry other malfeasances, I will say nothing. What concerns us now is the hippie age.

What Kennedy's death, the war in Viet-Nam's escalation and the slow pace of change (so called) did not do was to destroy the optimism of the younger generation of that time. It did destroy its conventional appearance. What emerged from the anti-war struggle, the disaffection with mainstream American values, and the search for a new meaning for life was... the hippie movement.

I suppose that anyone much younger than I (and I am only 26, in this fun-filled year of 1987) will not be able to remember those days. But they were wild times. Haight-Ashbury's Summer of Love in 1967, Berkeley and the free speech movement. Chicago riots, 1968. And more music: "If you're going to San Francisco... be sure to put some flowers in your hair." The first television generation had grown with the need to be entertained, a need to be excited, a need to be amused. This new set of T.V. inspired wants, coupled with the great material well-being of the time, and the decline of Protestant values produced some unfortunate occurences, to say the least. The discovery of narcotics, the abandonment of sexual mores, and the general debasement of the arts can hardly be called happy results.

Nevertheless, it is an ill wind that blows no one any good,

and many positive or potentially positive things did emerge from the sixties. Many of the more stultifying elements in American culture were dissipated. American letters, music, and art did acquire a new sophistication. Our traditional puritan antipathy to the impractical (read "unprofitable") was greatly mitigated, and the long tyranny of the Enlightenment over our intellectual life was broken. It may well be argued that the sixties ushered in our current immorality; the reply must be that sterility is not a virtue, and that a cold Calvinistic moral structure breeds hypocrisy. We Americans in the eighties may be narcissistic, automated, debauched, drugged-out and superficial, but except for the facade of being "caring and sensitive," we are fairly free of hypocrisy.

The early seventies saw the apparent abdication from virtue of our government through the affair of Watergate, and its actual abdication through the legalisation of abortion. The Viet-Nam war ended, as did Viet-Nam (its present ghost existence as a Soviet slave state is hardly real life.) The great causes died, although feminism, gay rights, busing, and the search for Jimmy Hoffa continued to occupy the hearts and minds of those with nothing better to do. Another Jimmy, this one from Georgia, ascended the sacred eminence of Presidential power, and dispensed wisdom in the form of pronouncing his lust for Poles. O beloved Seventies! Had you not been foreordained you would have been necessary to invent! Pointless, purposeless, you saw the emergence of legalised baby slaughter (though I believe your kid sister the Eighties perfected using the little corpses for commercial beauty aids and shampoos.) Win buttons and pet rocks. Mood rings and Perrier. And the seemingly endless days of the Iranian hostage situation whilst Jimmy fought for the Moral High Ground. The decade ended not with a bang, but a snicker.

Nineteen eighty saw the election of Ronald Reagan, who epitomises at once the old American Values, and the glamour of Hollywood. He is a man worth examining for several reasons. Although the oldest President we have ever had, he captured sixty-four percent of the youth vote in his reelection bid in 1984.

Under his predecessor Nicaragua, Grenada and Afghanistan became Communist, while Iran went mad, or perhaps took out a collective membership in Tom Hayden's CED. Yet under Reagan, not one country has fallen. Grenada was even freed. Did his thundering reelection of three years ago represent a new Conservatism? Yes and no.

Reagan has restored American prestige abroad, and improved the economy tremendously from the ruin Jimmy Dearest wrought. These portions of his program are tremendously popular. Not so his social policies. Most Americans favour abortion (it is to be supposed that this is because it "gives the woman the power of choice over her uterus" - as we have mentioned, Americans love the idea of free choice.)

The reason for this dichotomy is that we appreciate increased wealth. In the utopia of the 1980's, technology has produced more methods of gratifying the senses than have ever existed before. All the unpleasantness of life can be tuned out for a while. Videos, MTV, and the new music soothe tremendously. Money gives us the power to achieve all our parents strived for and subconsciously assures us that we are among the elect, as good old John Calvin would have said. Thus Reagan's election does not presage a moral renaissance; it does underline the present state of society.

As we have said, gratification is the reason which justifies what we children of plenty do. Marijuana, cocaine and other drugs are completely accepted by us young folk because they are pleasant and there is no societal pressure against them. Sexually, we are an exceeding permissive generation. Due to contraception and abortion, any real consequence of what was once called "illicit intercourse" is removed. Sex becomes a recreation like any other, the sexual partner no more than any other tool for pleasure. In more affluent and advanced circles, bisexuality is gaining acceptance. Why not? If frequent normal sex begins to bore, and the whole thing has only a pleasure value, does it matter who or what one's partner is?

Thus emerges the patron saint of the 1980's, the so-called

Yuppie. He or she is young, well-paid, on the way up. Independent, self-sufficient, he or she may do what he or she wants. Continued economic growth, of course, will provide the funds for their lifestyle. They may take, sleep with or use whatever they like, and only their own needs determine what is right for them. They must need be dedicated only to themselves, and so, even in a crowd, they are alone. Occasionally they will have to face themselves, and if sex, drugs and rock and roll will not make them happier, they have recourse to our old friend cheap thought. Political causes and self-help courses are comforting but undemanding religions. Immediately one thinks of the great Rev. Terry Cole-Whittaker, high priestess of what that infallible oracle, the L.A. "Weekly" calls the "affluhip." Alas, even Rev. Terry had to "transition to a high energy environment," and decamp to Hawaii to escape the pressures of being the yuppie archguruess. But many other prophets of non-responsibility remain, willing to say that one may do anything one wants to, and God will bless one for doing it.

The flip side of this is punk. Punk is essentially a rebellion against meaninglessness. But while one may parody and ridicule the ridiculous sacred cows of society, and mourn one's own outcast nature, one must have an alternative. The punks do not.

There is to our generation a nihilism: that is, a nothingism. For us, there are no absolutes, no morals, no vices and no virtues. We have been raised to believe that our own desires are the only goals we need. But it is not so. We have been taught that all desires can come true. But that is a lie. Our unachievable quest for constant gratification becomes a mere flight from pain that is as unrealistic as it is useless. That flight can go only into a dead end. Contrary to what our mentors, either at home or on the boob tube, have said, there is no happiness without responsibility, and there is no responsibility without pain.

All the striving and desire of our generation, which is surely as intense and fevered as any that have crawled upon this earth, has been misdirected. Only God can provide happiness. And God can only be truly and fully experienced in the Catholic

Church. It is not just the fact that the Church's moral code is at once reasonable and upright, or that honest attempts to follow her authentic teachings will create honourable individuals, capable of withstanding great suffering or of appreciating great joy. If that were all, one might benefit as well from reading Amy Vanderbilt as from being Catholic. It is the fact that only through her teaching, and through the Seven Sacraments that Christ ordained can one directly and physically experience God, and thus obtain Salvation.

The burning message of Christ, purveyed by the Catholic Church, is the answer to that longing on the part of our peers. Not yuppieism, which feeds the body, tans it and trims it, but starves the soul. Not politics, which rejects (in our case) any authority over the individual. Not fundamentalism, which substitutes dead interpretation of scripture and hymn-singing for the living Flame of the Holy Ghost. There is not a segment of our culture which would not benefit from the Faith. As far as creativity goes, is it not peculiar how many of our most avant-garde writers go to New Orleans, Taos, or the south of France, where the memory of Catholic culture still lingers? In truly Catholic ambiences dwells that which inflames the hearts of men.

Given the situation in America herein described, it is to be thought that the Church would convert the United States as she did Rome, though more swiftly, because of modern communications. Surely their lordships the bishops would sweep through the land, proselyting the cardboard people, making them real men, sons of God, as did the apostles? No such luck. The robbery described in the beginning of this book is perhaps as much the robbery from our non-Catholic compadres of any real evangelisation, as it is of our heritage from us.

You will recall that we left their lordships happy during the reign of good King John. But there was at that time another John sitting upon another throne - Pope John XXIII. He had expressed a desire for aggniormento - for an updating of the Church, to deal with the modern world. Given the problems of Communism, the new technology and the general modern sickness, the Church had to prepare for a great burst of energy to conquer this brave new world for Christ. Thus did the aged pope hope for a "new Pentecost," and to that end called for a new council of the Church - Vatican II.

To describe the manner in which the council was highjacked, the skullduggery that went on the part of the Modernists, would take a larger book than this. Suffice it to say that the council produced a ton of documents, none of which, except the Decree on Religious Liberty, were too bad in themselves. But the periti, the experts (theological bureaucrats and postal clerks - apologies to those professions) had planted all sorts of ambiguous phrases in the documents. As they were the bureaucracy of the Church, they would carry out the decrees of the council in a manner to suit their own tastes. And those tastes ran to Modernism and Communism. At least they ran to the destruction of the Church.

A strong pope could have kept things on line. Paul VI was not such a pope. Committed, doctrinal, zealous bishops could have stood up. Their American lordships were not, for the most part, such bishops. They allowed the various diocesan committees to seize their spiritual power. Of course, My Lords kept control of diocesan finances.

Over a period of six years the bishops, against the wishes of the vast majority of their laity, transformed the sublime ceremonial of the Mass, which exemplified the awful reality of the mystery taking place, into a celebration of community. They took the new Mass, which Paul VI perhaps mistakenly promulgated, and translated and revised it to their own lack of taste. Of course, they were aided by Modernists in the Curia. They illegally outlawed the old Mass, and gave heavy penalties to any Priest daring enough to offer it. In short, they were able to conform completely to the great culture around them. They redesigned Catholic Churches to show that Christ the King was dethroned, by moving the tabernacle to an inconspicuous place. They introduced communion in the hand, had the Priest face the people, imported bad music, indeed, did anything possible to make the Mass unlike a sacrifice to God. Why not? Had not

American society done well by pursuing man instead of God? Surely we would at least be popular! The war with Satan made so few friends, in comparison to the war on poverty.

Catholic education, already carefully secure from anything which could offend non-Catholics, must be de-Catholicised completely. The young must have the same beliefs as their mainstream counterparts. The doctrine which leads to temporal happiness and eternal life must be banished, lest Catholics lay themselves open to the charge of being different. Absolutes must be replaced with uncertainties, morals with growth. And it was done.

In 1968, Pope Paul VI, that great believer in the power of thought over action, wrote a truly great encyclical, "Humanae Vitae," which reaffirmed the Church's ban on birth control (artificial, that is). He correctly pointed out what would result from the use of contraception. Abortion, euthanasia, and the progressive dehumanization of man. In this he was a better prophet than their Lordships who, after consulting tarot cards, horoscopes, tealeaves, and Folger's Coffee Crystals, divined that neither their stricken flocks nor (more importantly) mainstream public opinion would be pleased by the pope's pronouncement. Did they rally round the document, showing its reason and clarity? No. They clammed up, and allowed their more progressive theologians and lackeys to attack it with impunity.

Yet another part of My Lord's attempt to be popular was ecumania. In truth, the biggest difference between Protestants and Catholics is this: Catholics believe that the Church is the living body of Christ, administering the sacraments of grace, dispensing the unchanging doctrine of Christ, and headed by the successor of St. Peter, the rock upon which Christ said His Church was founded. To that Church unquestioning obedience must be given, in the sphere of Faith and morals. Protestants believe that the Church is a gathering of individuals committed to studying the scriptures and encouraging each other in the practise of a "good life." If one disagrees with the teaching of one church, he may find another, for "no one has a monopoly of truth." This model of belief accorded well with the American spirit, which tends to reject authority and exclusiveness. Moreover, much is left to the whim of the individual clergyman, since he has as much autonomy as his layfolk. So, their Lordships found in ecumenism a marvellous pretext for refashioning the Catholic Church in America to a less "foreign," less difficult to monopolise pattern. In addition, the ecumenical recognition of the Protestant sects as having equal validity with the Church absolved the bishops of their divinely decreed mandate to spread the Faith. Are not nearly all Americans Christians of some sort? And are not those remaining non-Christians also seeking God? Or at least trying to be good?

Lastly, from 1964 to the present, they have tried to be "trendier than thou." There is no cause which they will not put their steadily diminishing authority on, as long as it be Liberal enough. Were the media Conservative, they would doubtless be so also. They pay lip service to the anti-abortion issue, while doing nothing concrete to stop the murder.

According to Cardinal Gagnon, the pro-President of the Pontifical Commission on the Family, most of the American bishops are in material schism. While there have been a few, like James Francis Cardinal McIntyre, who have attempted to remain loyal to the Church, most have been either too evily intentioned or too lazy or too cowardly to act as bishops should.

Those priests and nuns who did not agree with the new regime were quietly put aside, or else held their tongues, trying to do what good they could in a small way. But most actively promoted the new order, foisting the most anti-Catholic things on the people under their care.

What of the layfolk, our beloved parents? Long accustomed to taking the clergy's word for everything, committed to making a niche for themselves (and us), they were not concerned. Those who became concerned usually did so too late. In any case, bingo was still held, raffles were announced, just as if nothing had happened. Besides, the new things were easier. Why humble yourself in the confessional? Why strain yourself to comprehend the Mass, as though it was more to the glory of God than to make us feel better about ourselves? Why eat fish on Friday? The kids? Oh, yeah, they'll be Catholic, just like us. Aren't they going to Catholic school? Sister will teach them their religion.

But Sister did not teach us our religion, because Sister had lost hers. And we were turned out among the wolves of this world, without our Faith. Deprived of that Faith which alone brings eternal life, how many of us will escape hell? And are not those men monsters who brought this about? In a civilised age, perhaps, some of those bishops and theologians would have been burned. The Church in America is a gutted ruin, not only incapable of converting our native land, but also of holding our allegiance. I feel now like an elfish minstrel, strumming his harp, looking over the wreck evil Morgoth made of hidden city of Gondolin in Tolkien's *Silmarillion*.

But Christ promised his Church would last forever, and -- Hark! I hear trumpets. From far Cracow, in Poland, has come a liberator to rescue Holy Mother Church! It is our new pope, John Paul II. Already, he has allowed the return of the old Mass (in such a way as to very politically allow the bishops to avoid having to admit that they swindled us!) He has reaffirmed the teachings of the Church, and he is gearing up for the struggle with the powers that be for the future of Catholicism in America.

But as he expressed through his "Big Three," Cardinals Oddi, Ratzinger, and Gagnon, he needs the help of the laity; he needs our help. We are the future, and we must ensure that the future is Catholic. We must assist in the reconversion of the American Church, and undo the damage done by six generations of weakness, compromise and treason. Then we must turn our sights onto the fulfillment of Christ's mandate in regard to the U.S.A. We must first taste for ourselves, and then give to our peers that liberty in Christ which alone can statisfy us on this Earth, and save us in the next world.

We are done singing of the past. In the next section, we shall deal with concrete steps for fulfilling the task set before us. If enough of us follow them, then we shall be like the Apostles and other early Catholics, who set the known world at Christ's feet, despite the power of Persia and Rome. With such a King as Christ, such a Queen as Mary, such a Pope as John Paul II, even defeat in this cause would be sweet.

The cause ahead of us then, is true liberation, from Liberalism, from Protestantism, from Communism and Modernism, from the spirit of this world. May we sing as did the Irish in 1798, "We are the boys of Wexford, who fought with heart and hand, to burst in twain the galling chain, and free our native land."

# III - LIVING WITH HERESY

# Purgation or
# The Catholic Miracle Diet

Just as immigrants to the United States eventually give up their barbarous customs and learn to follow the civilised American pursuits of tax dodging, wife-swapping and disco, so too, as we have seen, have we Catholics. But just as the fourth or fifth generation often regains its ethnic identity (at least enough to, say, dance the babushka at the annual Ruritanian American anchovy festival) so too must we. It is more than just regaining contact with our roots, raising our consciousness, or learning to make West African savoury goo. It is overcoming generations of cheap thought, shoddy logic, popularity seeking, and weakness on the part of our Catholic forebears, our clergy, and most of all, our selves. It involves that difficult act, made so hard by our upbringing, our culture and our own ingrained attitudes: the act of being true. True to our God in following His Will, and His alone, as expressed in the authentic teaching of His Church. True to ourselves, in being and doing that which we were created for, and only in which we can be truly happy.

It follows, then, that before we can do anything constructive, we must rid ourselves of certain mental preconditioning bequeathed to us by the factors mentioned above. Of all the generations ever spawned in this land of the free and home of the brave, ours has been the most nourished by lies. Falsehood throbs, pumps and flows through our thought. Getting everything we want will make us happy. Sex will make us happy. Drugs will make us happy. We alone can determine what is right for us. If only we push hard enough, total freedom and total indulgence will bring total joy. We have been sold a bill of spoiled goods, and for lack of learning, wisdom, or age, we have bought them.

We are grown ups, now, so we must take responsibility. It is time to put down the coke spoon and the joint, time to have our lover dressed and out the door, time to turn off MTV (for a little while! Far be it from me to dictate musical taste, but your attention is required!), time to forget the advice (but not of course, the affection) of our friends. None of them will bring lasting happiness. So let us begin our work.

The first thing we must realise is the fact already alluded to, that this world is a world full of lies. Truth, loyalty and honour are mere buzz words. Love is a myth, and trust a fallacy. The reason for this is that these qualities are naturally only to be found in their (and our) Creator. God is many things, but among them He is the perfect gathering of all virtues. He created men and angels to share His boundless love with them; He endowed them with free-will, to return that love freely. When, with Adam's fall, man showed his rejection of God, God did not desert man, as a man would have. No indeed, He watched with man through the years of the Old Testament. At length, He Himself became incarnate, and bled and died, and sent His Holy Spirit, and created His Holy Church, all to guide men to him. In that Church He provided, through His sacraments, and His teaching, the way for man to escape the effects of his nature. All the virtues were ennobled by that Church; when most men rejected that Church, they rejected God, and those virtues began to die.

The first step we must take, then, is submission. We must submit our wills to that of God, to His Church. We must lose our American phobia against authority. What the Church teaches is what God teaches; there is no distinction. If the Church taught that the moon is made of green cheese and takes its ease at Casey's bar of a Thursday night, we must believe it. The world, as it is, is the result of following our own ideas. We cannot, as John Lennon asked, "give peace a chance," until we give God and his Church a chance. So let us resolve then, that we shall give up our will to the Church, that we seek not our pleasure, but God's. If we do not, we set ourselves up as superior to God, we repeat Satan's fall, and we share his fate. And Hell is just not worth it.

Now then, it is important (indeed essential) to reorganise our lives, morally speaking, in accordance with the Church's teaching. This will require sacrifice, but then, what did Christ do for us? If I do what the Church condemns, I must acknowledge first that I, and not the Church, am wrong, I must break my pride. I must strive against temptation. But I must never forget that I can do nothing without God's help, and that I have always His love.

If one lives with a person of the opposite sex, without marriage, then they must either marry or separate. One may not indulge in sex outside of marriage, nor use contraception inside of it. One may not indulge in homosexuality, nor have an abortion. This is easy enough to say, but not so easy to do, depending on the individual and his or her circumstances. But one must try, never giving up the fight, no matter how long it takes, or how many times one might fall. In the battle against habitual serious sin, one must get out of oneself. Involvement in Catholic organisations, frequent reception of confession and communion, and good friendships will help immensely.

One must try to inculcate in oneself all of the virtues that one admires. Honour, self-sacrifice, loyalty; all of these things we desire in others, we must first show in ourselves. Then, perhaps, they will show themselves in others.

If we seek God, truth, and the will of the Church above all else, sparing neither our own comfort, or other's regard for us, we will find all that we truly desire, all that the world, the flesh, and the devil promise, but cannot give. And in that battle, both interior and exterior, we will find salvation.

# Taking Problems to the Top

Before we may even think of donning armour, mounting our horses and riding against the foe, we must get orders. We must talk to the Boss. In other words, we must learn to pray.

The primary method of prayer is to be found in the sacraments. Since we are not perfect, since we are sinful, what better way to make amends to God than confession, which He Himself has ordered? In return for real repentance, we will experience for ourselves Christ's power of forgiveness. Whatever evil we have done, it can vanish immediately. Whatever our sins, through confession, we may become as innocent as babies. Frequent confession, then, is a marvellous way to communicate with Our Lord.

Still more marvellous, though, is the Mass. The reception of Our Lord in His living Body and Blood, Soul and Divinity, is to communicate with Him in a manner so intimate, so close, that nothing in human terms can equal it. Sexual contact is perhaps, (when it is accompanied by true love and devotion) the closest that two individuals may become. But it might as well be that the husband and wife are at the opposite poles in comparison to the union between Christ and the believer in the Eucharist. We humans know instinctively that we are cut off and alone, and that this is unnatural. But we can only get so close to another person, and no further. As we were created for loving union with our Creator, it follows that that union is the unconscious model for all of our relationships. In the Eucharist, that real and total union we hunger for occurs, and fills us with life. The lack of that union is eternal death.

It is no coincidence that the poetry attempting to describe this action, written about by the great mystics, reads like the most intense love poetry. How could they be otherwise, seeing that they describe the most intense love this universe knows?

Freud declared that much religious devotion was misplaced sexuality. Jung believed that much sexuality was misplaced religious devotion. If ever a time and a society proved his dictum, it is ours. Loving God will then not only procure our salvation, but free us from psychiatric bills.

It is to be granted that the Liturgical changes foisted upon us by their Lordships the Bishops have deprived the Mass of much of its sublime appearance, of its devotional attraction. But there are ways around that problem.

In some dioceses, the more survival-minded bishops have grudgingly complied with the pope's new indult, and established occasional Tridentine Masses. In addition, certain priests, without the authorisation of the local bishop, also offer the old Mass. When wondering about the legitimacy of such Masses, one must remember that, as Cardinal Oddi has said, any Mass of an authorised Catholic rite fills the Sunday obligation. Some caution must be exercised, however, since some "Traditionalist" priests belong to movements which are, to say the least, peculiar. If the priest in question (a) does not believe that John Paul II is indeed the Pope, (b) does not allow any outside his own flock to receive communion at his Mass, or (c) does not believe in the validity of the Novus Ordo Mass - quite apart from thinking it inferior or suspect, then he is just as materially schismatic as the lords bishops mostly try to be. It is a thin line.

In a few specially favoured cities exists an interesting experiment: The Anglican use of the Catholic Church. This consists of priests and laymen who left the Episcopal Church for the Catholic due to the ordination of priestesses and sundry other weirdnesses our own Liberals would like to inflict on us. These refugees from the twilight zone of Modernism were granted in the U.S. (those in Britain and elsewhere await the same safe harbour, and meanwhile flounder in the outer darkness) an adaptation of their liturgy, which is essentially an English Tridentine Mass (and good English at that!) and conveys the mystery of the action. In addition, the high level of education and devotion to the Holy Father rampant among them make them very pleasant and orthodox companions. Since reception of their parishes has been made dependent upon the whim of the local bishop, it is a safe bet that they will not expand rapidly, so long as their lordships do not wish to expand the Church's size, to the detriment of their lordships' dear friends in the Episcopal Church.

Much more widespread are the Eastern rite churches. These come in a bewildering number of varieties (Ukranian, Maronite, Melkite, Chaldean, etc.) While very foreign to the Latin Catholic and to each other, they nevertheless surround the sacrament of the altar with beauty, mystery, and the aura of authentic Catholicism. Their priests are usually more Orthodox than many of our New Age clergy.

In a few places, the Novus Ordo can be heard in Latin (rather than the mistranslated English), and in fewer still can be seen the way the rubrics direct, complete with the priest's back to the people, facing toward God. This is rare, but when present one is not subjected to the onslaught of the cheap and banal.

What if none of these alternatives are available, what must one do? Grit one's teeth, and go to what is available. The important thing, in the final analysis, is Union with Our Lord. Of course, we can kneel, when we can; receive Our Lord on the tongue; dodge the Eucharistic Ministers and get to the priest, whose hands alone are consecrated; refuse the Wine, unless the priest himself holds the Chalice. We can offer Our Lord our love, and hope it diverts His eyes from the sacriligious shindigs indulged in so often by His worshipers, and His ears from the clanging and clacking of would be rock stars.

Another wise practise is to pray whatever one can of the "Divine Office," or the "Liturgy of the Hours." This is the official daily prayer of the Church, used in different forms by the various orders of religious. From Matins at three in the morning, to Compline at nine at night, the Church has a period of prayer set aside every three hours. Especially in its pre-liturgical stupefaction form, the Hours are a treasure house of prayers, psalms, and lessons from the oldest and most Catholic sources. While it is important to pray on one's own, prayer in union with the Church is the most effective. Even if one finds it impossible (as most laymen must) to pray the Hours in sequence, still it instills the spirit of Catholicism in the individual in a concrete manner. Doubtless our priests and bishops would also benefit from the practise, but the needs of the feminists, gays, peace movement folks and vegetable rights people naturally take precedence in their more Liberal lordships' and reverences' minds. After all, deep prayer-lives do not get one laudatory comments in "Mother Jones" or the "Nation."

The Rosary and Scapular must also be employed. At Fatima, in fact, Our Lady declared them to be our main hope. Cultivation of devotion to Our Lady is extremely important, as he who slights the mother slights the son. In this connection, however, one must be warned about so-called "apparitions" of Our Lady. Those approved by the Church have been rigourously examined and pronounced genuine; these the faithful Catholic is bound to learn about, as the Mother of God does not drop by the earth merely to make chit-chat. Those the Church has reserved judgement upon, we too must be silent about. Those she has condemned, we must condemn. But it is important to be loyal to Our Lady, in the manner prescribed by St. Louis de Montfort.

Devotion to Our Lord in the Eucharist outside of Mass is also important. Christ does not vanish after Mass. The priest may go to the golf course, have lunch with Protestant ministers and Jewish rabbis or attend an anti-nuke demonstration, but Our Lord stays with His people in the Tabernacle. He cannot, in that form, make parish calls as many of His priests would, were their time not so valuable, but His subjects can visit Him in His palaces that His ordained servants have for the most part looted and ransacked. He is left off to the side (for the Priest's chair now occupies in many places the spot from which He reigned) in a new tabernacle that is often as cheap as the old one was grand, genuflected to by none, except a few old half-senile ladies rattling their beads with more devotion often than the pastor shows at his principal Mass; there is no sign to show the presence of the King other than a sickly red lamp; He must live again His loneliness in the garden. Can we not visit with Him, share our personal minor problems with Him, and try to compensate Him by our love for all the agonies inflicted upon Him by sinners (ourselves included) and now compounded by those who bear the mark of His apostles?

His Saints also are deserving of honour. Residents of heaven, examples to us, indeed, older brothers in a sense, they too will pray to Our Lord on our behalf. The angels as well would like our spiritual company, as would certainly the suffering souls in Purgatory, who will pray for us if we pray for them. Indeed, as most of us who manage to escape hell will doubtless land there, it would be wise to pray for those whose punishment we may well share. For all of these companions on the way to God have devotions been developed, and despite what our pastor may say (who is often not sure if prayer to God Himself is heard, but who is devoted to the spirit of collection envelopes and bingo games,) we would do well to use them.

Personal prayer and meditation too are essential, especially if we are to be soldiers of Christ the King. We must try to be aware of the promptings of the Holy Ghost, but we must always temper what we hold to be divine stirrings with the accepted and authentic teaching of the Church.

It may be that you are lucky enough to be near a priest who is faithful to Christ and to the Church. He is probably either a retired priest, an overaged curate, or a pastor in a remote area. He is not likely to be newly ordained (unless very exceptional, and discrete enough to fool his teachers at his Modernist seminary), a Pastor of a wealthy parish, or a Chancery official. There are exceptions, however. If you do know such a one, get him as your own confessor and spiritual director, pronto! He is worth his weight in gold, and may be either nearing 90 or awaiting transfer to St. Frigida's in Timbuktoo. You will learn more about true devotion to Our Lord from him than you ever will from this book. If he is strictly orthodox, mitigates the abuses of the Mass as much as possible, encourages the Rosary, Scapular, novenas and the like, loves to hear confessions, visits the sick and makes parish calls, then he is your man. He will be humble, and will genuinely care for you (not by words, which mean nothing, but by taking the time to direct your prayer life). In short, he will earn your respect not merely by his collar, but by his words and deeds. You will learn why priests are called "Father."

It may be objected that one has little time for prayer. Perhaps, but it is amazing how often one can find time for one's favorite T.V. show. Even the "Twilight Zone" (my own preference) cannot guarantee salvation.

The more one becomes a man or woman of prayer, the closer he or she resembles Christ. It is the hallmark of the Liberal that he believes man can improve his world without changing himself. This is the essential error he makes. Let us not be fooled. It was prayer that made the saints holy, it was prayer that gave them miracles, and it was prayer that allowed them to conquer the world for Christ. If we wish to free our Church and our country from the evil ideas and the evil men who enslave them, we must first become people of prayer. Otherwise, it would merely be a case of substituting one set of scoundrels for another, of corrupt young fools for corrupt old fools. Are not most (if not all) political revolutions like that? The only method of avoiding becoming the mirror images of the enemy is that of prayer, penance and humilty.

But prayer without study will make a holy man, not an informed one. Although a number of the saints have carried the title "A fool for Christ's sake," there is no need to be foolish on our own account. Study without prayer leads to pride. With the field of the mind prepared for tilling by prayer, we will sow the seed of learning in the next chapter.

# To Be a Know-It-All
# or
# Showing Up Father

The combat we are engaged upon is in great part a battle over information. Our whole outlook has been formed by what we saw on T.V., by what we were taught in school and by what our parents, family and friends said and did. We live in a society of specialists, and those specialists have become the witch doctors of today. While this is necessary in the more technological fields, it is disastrous in the field of religion. It is astounding that those priests who use only the worst English possible in the Mass, use the purest Latin when trying to impress layfolk with their knowledge. They attempt to mystify and to impress in order to misinform. But often their knowledge of doctrine, liturgy, and history is quite scanty. Psychology they know, sociology, pastoral counseling and finance, all these they are masters of. But those things that most concern their sacred calling? Well, the seminary had tons of electives on Marx, Mohammed, the modern philosophy. Aquinas and Augustine were covered with twenty-five other orthodox, heretical, pagan, Jewish, and Moslem thinkers in a single survey course. If one is to resist their nonsense, one must know more than they.

To this end we are including a handy guide for study. If faithfully adhered to, you will become a walking treasury of facts, able to win games of trivial pursuit, to annoy family and friends alike, and to impress the easily impressed. Most important, you will be able to show up Fr. Liberal for the phony he is. Perhaps even his superior, Cardinal Bogus (though I doubt my lord cardinal would notice or care about anything short of a loss in diocesan revenues, or golf game lost to his pal, the Episcopal bishop) would take notice, scurrying between bishop's conferences at swanky resorts.

If you went to Catholic school, chances are you were mistaught. If in high school (or at any time) you used a book called "Christ Among Us" you definitely were. So we must start with a course of doctrine. First must come a basic catechism. Then must come the infallible creeds, councils, and Papal definitions. If one wants to go further into the fathers, doctors, an definitions. If one wants to go further into the fathers, doctors, and great theologians of the Church, one must always judge them against a background of revealed Catholic dogma. There is an old saying that "every doctor of the Church has at least one error in his writings to show that the Pope alone is infallible." Indeed, in a private capacity even Popes have erred (although they never taught those errors as head of the Church, binding on all men on pain of heresy and hell). It is essential then to lay down a foundation of revealed truth, before bothering with speculation. Beware, however, of theologians who try to "interpret, nuance, or rethink," infallible statements. Had Pope or Council meant something different from what they clearly said, they would have said something else. Often this "nuancing" is done to remove uncomfortable doctrine. But if the doctrine is uncomfortable, it is the theologian who must be "nuanced."

Next comes history, both Church and secular. We were not grounded well enough in it in school, especially not in Church History. Even the presentation in this book is much too generalised to be of any use apart from giving a broad impression. History is essential because it allows us to understand the present and, to a degree, the future. It brings perspective for instead of swooning when one hears Fr. Liberal preaching heresy, one will merely think, "My, Fr. Liberal is an Arian. That heresy was refuted at the Council of Nicea!" - and then go back to sleep. It consoles us with thoughts of times that were worse than these and yet overcome by the Church. It encourages us by stories of great victories reserved for those who were steadfast. In addition, the lives of the saints give us examples to follow, of individuals in equal or worse times.

Liturgy too must be studied. In order to understand the

nature of the changes our faithful shepherds foisted upon us, we must familiarise ourselves with the development of the Mass, the rationale behind its ceremonies and the variety of rites practised with it. To understand the present confusion of the liturgy, one should study the encyclicals of Popes Pius XII, John XXIII, Paul VI, and John Paul II, especially the last which deal with Liturgy. If you do, you will have done more and know more about the authentic mind of the Church on this matter than your parish liturgical committee. Of course, they are more concerned with being progressive, by which they mean a return to the spirit of the 1960's.

Mention of the sixties calls attention to social matters. Today, since peasants are in short supply in America, the disguises used by the then bishops to desert Boniface VIII would be useless. Thus, their modern descendants use the guises of social worker and peace advocate to escape their rightful role. One then must study the social teachings of the Church, which alone can provide real social and economic peace for our country. The oligarchic technocracy (try saying that phrase nine time backwards!) which runs the United States now is as morally bankrupt as the Marxist colossus, its nominal opponent. It would seem that the bishops, in their haste to be trendier-than-thou, are in reality attempting to follow the policy of compromise that so many of their predecessors followed, in order to preserve the privilege and position of the Church when our present system mutates into something else, or is overcome by the Communists. But this is policy, dubious at best, which worked only when the powers-that-were were Catholic.

In short, we young Catholics must prepare ourselves, by means of prayer and study, to be instruments of Christ's Will, as expressed by His Vicar, the Pope. Without this preparation we will be unable to act. The Second Vatican Council called upon the lay folks to exercise our unique apostolate. And so we must, if our rebellious lords and bishops, and their attendant Liberal clergy are not to destroy the Church in America.

# Keeping His Lordship
# Off the Streets
## or
# Catching Up with the Crusades

The much maligned but extremely perceptive priest, Fr. Charles Coughlin, wrote in his under-read (perhaps because true) book *Bishops versus the Pope* on p. 73,

> Pius XII was very conscious of this epidemic of disaster which is befalling the Church. Instead of naming it, he referred to it in his Encyclical Humani Generis as 'the new philosophy of total error.' In a sense it is not a philosophy. Rather it is an ideological harem where are congregated the frowsy concubines in the fields of theology, philosophy, liturgy, Scripture, and metaphysics, all of whom take turns in disavowing conventionality, reviving ancient errors and, in one manner or the other, assailing all the Apostolic truths of Catholicity. Overlording them is the gentle Jesuit, de Chardin.

It is the heresy, the synthesis of all heresies, as St. Pius X put it, of Modernism which has infected the Church in America today. It is this that we were taught in school that was served up to us in the altered Mass. This nightmare of nebulosity, of confusion, which reduces God, in the end, to that entity described by the great Lovecraft, as "Azathoth, the great idiot-god who gibbers senselessly in the centre of eternity, to the piping of insane flutes." It is this creature whom the new theologians would like to place on the throne of Heaven. And this is only just, for Azathoth mirrors the diabolic emptiness in the depths of these theologian's souls. No longer do they dare to say God is dead - instead they say that He and His Church are senile and do not understand modern life.

In this they are assisted by the media. These modern prophets do their best to discredit the teachings of the Church as antique. Most interesting is the high number of media personages who, while non-Catholics, or ex-Catholics, demonstrate an infallibility superior to the Pope.

Catholic politicians such as Mario Cuomo, Jerry Brown, or Geraldine Ferraro, who use their nominal membership in the Church to get votes and yet deny the primacy of the Church's moral teaching, constitute the third facet of the unholy alliance which keeps the American Church in bondage. The best commentary upon this brood of vipers is the resounding defeat of Mrs. Ferraro-Zaccaro's vice-presidential campaign in her own district. Would that New Yorkers as a whole showed such under standing with Cuomo, or Bay Staters with Senator Kennedy.

Of course, the struggle with these odious creatures ought to be directed by those whom God and the Holy See have placed over us - our chiefs, our shepherds, our fathers-under-God; their Lordships, Graces and Eminences, the American bishops. As we have seen, most of them have betrayed their God-given trust through compromise, pride and self will. But far be it for me to call them evil. As Fr. Coughlin (who for his prophetic ability alone should be rehabilitated, as many of the Red Chinese presently in leadership were after Mao's death closed the book on the Cultural Revolution) points out on page 1 of "Bishops versus the Pope,"

> Bishops are not judged by the so-called immor-
> alities common to other men. As a rule, they are too
> old to be fornicators or adulterers. As a matter of
> fact, it is seldom one of them is to be classified as a
> thief or a character assasin. For the most part, they
> are mild, charitable gentlemen who enjoy their
> millinery as they sit on the episcopal throne and take
> pleasure in the adulation bestowed upon them by
> Catholic and Protestant, Jew and gentile. Prudence
> is one of their chief virtues even though it sometimes
> degenerates into criminal prudence. Propriety is

their outer garment of conduct. Affability is their charm but, regretful as it is, one would think that a law had been passed, relative to concealed weapons when one considers how adroitly and expertly so many of them hide the Sword of the Spirit. It is a sword instituted by the Blessed Trinity and placed in the hands of all Bishops to enable them to battle for truth and not to seek to survive for survival's sake.

But despite the lack, perhaps of evil intent, they are guilty for allowing the great robbery described earlier. They who should be leaders in the struggle are often neutral, or worse, obstructions to the work of the pope in evangelising the world and confirming us, the least of the brethren. We must keep this in mind when considering how best to proceed. We, who have no training, must act as crusaders and missionaries while his lordship is saving the whales, currying favour with Donahue's kindred or playing golf.

Having carefully prepared ourselves through prayer and study, we are now armed. We should read a number of Catholic periodicals (listed in the appendix - at no extra charge) to understand the current situation, both in our own area, throughout the nation and overseas.

Now comes the need for individual action. This will vary according to one's location, but it will consist primarily of teaching the Faith to the misinformed, the Protestant, the Jew, one's cronies, all in the most persuasive manner possible. It will include challenging heresy wherever it comes from, particularly with priests, nuns, and teachers. They in particular must be made to account for whatever nonsense they spout. The list of possibilities is endless. One must be skillful for this work, so cultivate a deep devotion to the Holy Ghost. He will aid you.

There is, however, only so much the individual can do. One must reflect Catholicism in all one's doings, but one can only reach so far. So, it becomes important to join or form a group of like-minded people. Of course the particular emphasis in each group - political, social, devotional, or some combination of the three will differ. But as long as they are grounded in authentic Catholic doctrine, their sphere will be successful. We will put a list of organisations in the appendix as well.

In addition, there are mainstream Catholic organisations dedicated to one worthy cause or another. Membership in one or more of these (Knights of Columbus, Holy Name, etc.) is useful because it not only allows one to do good work, but also to spread true Catholicism among those likely to appreciate it. It is the lay people who are the strength and money of the Church. If organised to properly pressure the bishops to follow the pope's directives (such as the Tridentine Mass indult) then the Church here could finally tackle her real mission: to convert our fellow citizens to the path which will save their souls.

We must breed within ourselves a Sacramental view of life. We must realise that only the Faith will save our souls, make us authentic human beings, and bring meaning to this world of misery, pain and sin in which we live.

In conclusion, let us think of the old hymn:

> Our Fathers, chained in prisons dark,
>   Were still in heart and conscience free;
> How sweet would be their children's fate,
>   If they, like them, could die for thee!
>
> Faith of Our Fathers, Mary's prayers
>   Shall win our country unto thee:
> And through the truth that comes from God
>   Mankind shall then indeed be free.

# L'ENVOI
# OR
# THE AUTHOR'S FAREWELL
# TO HIS READERS

### I. TO HIS PEERS

Now, my friends, the story is told. But as you will understand from history, the story does not end, and will not until the Great Author closes the book. The times are dark, and we have been defrauded. As with every generation, we have a choice: to that for which we were created, and gain Heaven; or to our own will, and gain Hell. We are young, we are the future, so let us try to do better than our fathers. God bless you all, and Our Lady keep you.

### II. TO THE OLDER LAYMEN (AND WOMEN)

I have perhaps spoken roughly of you in the course of this book. Truly, of all the players in this little show, you were the least to blame. There is much you can do yet to right things. Become informed and active. With the power of the purse, you can collectively force change. Do it then, for the sake of those whose bodies you cared for, that we might not lose our souls.

### III. TO THE REVEREND FATHERS

You will doubtless believe that I am exceedingly impertinent in treating you as I have in this book. Perhaps I have been.

Perhaps I have been unjust. Certainly, I have known holy priests, whose teaching and examples have lighted my road. But these were loyal, plodding drudges, devoted to Our Lord and Our Lady, and Pope and Church, and their people. Not for them the new theology, chancery positions, startling books, and the world's acclaim. No, for them the endless round of parish calls, the sacraments and the spiritual and corporal works of mercy. They gave their people the means of unending life which only the Church provides, and many still do. But what of you New Wave theologians? What of you innovators, you prophets of do-it-yourself morality who laugh at the Pope's liturgical directives and snicker at his sexual ethics? Laugh while you may, but even if a good bishop does not punish you, or informed laymen refuse to pay you, you must face Our Lord. Think of that when you deny the Real Presence, or the Virgin Birth, when you call Benediction "cookie worship" or sneer at the Rosary. After death you will account for the souls you lost. But what a reward for you, what rejoicing in Heaven, if you leave Chardin, Rahner, and Co. to fry as they might and begin to teach orthodoxy and to offer the Mass (for which rite you exist) reverently. Think of the sheep and the goats, my dear biblical scholars. If you will not kneel before Our Lord in this life, you will grovel before Him in the next, to no avail.


## IV. TO THEIR LORDSHIPS THE BISHOPS

My lords, what I have said for the priests goes double for you. It was a holy cardinal whose kind advice and wise counsel kept me in the Faith. You who are the source of sacramental life have no right to do as you have done. Do not cause our Pope any more pain; preach the Faith, and defy the world, please. Or else just retire to nursing homes. God has given you greater graces than anyone else, so please use them.

## V. TO HIS HOLINESS THE POPE

Your Holiness, you have always had a special love of youth. Please come to the aid of your children in America. You know the situation here, you know what has happened to my generation. We must say to you, as did your predecessor to Our Lord, "Save us Master, or we perish." Your people drift and die, and only occassionally do we have a ray of hope from Rome. You alone may force the bishops to do God's will. Please do so, for the sake of us whom God has committed to your tender care.

## VI. TO ALL

Thank you, kind and gentle readers, for persevering to the end with me. I submit this book and all its contents to the judgment of the Holy Roman Church, whose obedient subject I am. I ask my readers to pray for my soul, as I will assuredly pray for theirs.

# STUDY GUIDE

As mentioned in the text, we here provide a guide to some important Catholic books. While nowhere near exhaustive, if one were to read all the books included, one would go far to absorbing the authentic Catholic ethos. All of them have bibliographies (if they are non-fiction) and will thus assist further research. While your faithful author may not agree with everything in them, he does not claim to be infallible himself, and so submits them to his loyal readers.

## I. RELIGIOUS BOOKS

The Bible, Douay-Rheims Version
Rockford, Illinois, TAN Books, 1971
(The only 100% accurate English version of the Old and New Testament)

The New Testament with full Catholic Commentary and an Illustrated and Comprehensive Catholic Bible Dictionary, Victory Publications, P.O. Box 80636, San Marino, CA 91108

Chateaubriand, Francois, Vicomte de
*The Genius of Christianity*
Paris, E. Thunut, 1854 403 pp.
(Recently reprinted)

Chesterton, G.K.,
*Orthodoxy*
Garden City, Doubleday, 1959 299 pp.

Cruz, Joan Carroll
*The Incorruptibles*
Rockford, Illinois, TAN Books 1977, 310 pp.

Cruz, Joan Carroll
*Relics*
Huntington, Indiana, OSV Press 1984 308 pp.

Feeney, Fr. Leonard
*Bread of Life*
Still River, MA., St. Benedict Center 1952, 204 pp.

Fox, Fr. Robert J.
*A Catechism of the Catholic Church*
Chicago, Franciscan Herald Press 1979, 247 pp.

Meagher, Fr. James L.
*How Christ Said the First Mass*
Rockford, Illinois TAN Books 1984, 438 pp.

Miceli, S.J., Fr. Vincent
*The Antichrist*
West Hanover, MA, Christopher Press 1984, 297 pp.

Sennott, Thomas Mary
*The Six Days of Creation*
Cambridge, MA, Ravengate Press 1984, 384 pp.

Sisters Adorers of the Precious Blood
*Saint Michael and the Angels*
Rockford, Illinois, TAN Books, 1983, 133 pp.

Vonier, Abbot
*Collected Works*
Westminster, MD, Newman Press, 1953, 3 vols.

## II. MODERN PROBLEMS

These books will reveal part of the nature of the struggle within the Church, give the reader the necessary information to carry on the battle, and inflame him to the urgency of the fight.

Cowden-Guido, Richard
*John Paul II and the Battle for Vatican II*
Manassas, VA 1986, Trinity Communications, 448 pp.

Coughlin, Fr. Charles E.
*Bishops versus the Pope*
Bloomfield, MI, Helmet and Sword 1969 220 pp.

Davies, Michael
*Cranmer's Godly Order*
Devon, Augustine 1977, 336 pp.

Davies, Michael
*Pope Paul's New Mass*
Devon, Augustine 1981, 673 pp.

Martin, Malachi
*The Jesuits*
New York, Simon and Schuster 1987

Muggeridge, Anne Roche
*The Desolate City*
San Francisco, Harper and Row 1986

Poncins, Leon, Vicomte de
*Freemasonry and the Vatican*
(Unknown) 1968 224 pp.

Wickens, Fr. Paul A.
*Christ Denied*
Rockford, Illinois, TAN books 1982, 48 pp.

## III. SOCIAL PROBLEMS

These books present various aspects of the social and political problems of our day from a strict Catholic viewpoint. While not applicable to all aspects of American life, they will stimulate thinking in new and fresh directions. Certainly, they do present a refreshing change from the tired political and social philosophies with which we have to deal.

Belloc, Hilaire
*The Servile State*
New York, H. Holt and Co., 1946, 188 pp.

Cahill, S.J., Fr. E.
*Freemasonry and the Anti-Christian Movement*
Dublin, M.H. Gill and Son 1949, 271 pp.

Correa de Oliveira, Plinio
*Revolution and Counter-Revolution*
New Rochelle, Foundation for a Christian Civilization 1980, 192 pp.

Dawson, Christopher
*Beyond Politics*
New York, Sheed and Ward 1939, 136 pp.

Fahey, C.S.Sp., Fr. Denis
*The Kingship of Christ and the Conversion of the Jewish Nation,*
Dublin, Holy Ghost Missionary College 1953, 192 pp.

Fahey, C.S.Sp., Fr. Denis
*The Mystical Body of Christ and the Reorganization of Society*
Dublin, Regina Publications, Ltd. 1978, 587 pp.

Fahey, C.S.Sp., Fr. Denis
*The Rulers of Russia*
(Unknown) 1984, 100 pp.

Fay, Bernard
*Revolution and Freemasonry, 1680-1800*
Boston, Little, Brown and Co. 1935, 349 pp.

Habsburg, Archduke Otto von,
*The Social Order of Tomorrow*
London, Wolff 1958, 158 pp.

Kirk, Russell
*The Conservative Mind: From Burke to Santayana*
Chicago, H. Regnery and Co., 1954, 478 pp.

Kuehnelt-Leddihn, Erik Maria, Ritter von
*Liberty or Equality, the Challenge of Our Time*
Caldwell, ID, Caxton Printers 1952, 395 pp.

Loewenstein-Scharffeneck, Hubertus, Prince zu
*After Hitler's Fall; Germany's Coming Reich*
London, Faber and Faber 1934, 281 pp.

Loewenstein-Scharffeneck, Hubertus, Prince zu
*Tragedy of a Nation; Germany 1918-1934*
New York, Macmillan 1934, 373 pp.

Machen, Arthur
*Dr. Stiggins: his views and principles*
New York, A.A. Knopf 1925, 202 pp.

Molnar, Thomas
*The Counter-Revolution*
New York, Funk and Wagnall 1969, 209 pp.

Novalis
*Christendom or Europe?*

Senior, John
*The Death of Christian Culture*
New Rochelle, Arlington House 1978, 185 pp.

Tyrrell, Jr., R. Emmett
*The Liberal Crack-Up*
New York, Simon and Schuster 1984, 256 pp.

## IV. HISTORICAL

As has been observed, we cannot know where we are until we know where we have been. Most history books in English are subtly or violently anti-Catholic. These should provide a partial antidote.

Belloc, Hilaire
*A Shorter History of England*
New York, Macmillan 1934, 675 pp.

Caroll, Dr. Anne
*Christ the King, the Lord of History*
Manassas, VA 1986, Trinity Communications

Belloc, Hilaire
*Characters of the Reformation*
New York, Sheed and Ward 1938, 342 pp.

Chambers, R.W.
*Thomas More*
London, Jonathan Cape Ltd. 1935, 416 pp.

Clayton, Joseph
*Pope Innocent III and His Times*
Milwaukee, Bruce Publishing Co. 1941, 204 pp.

Corvo, Frederick Rolfe, Baron
*Chronicles of the House of Borgia*
New York, E.P. Dutton Co. 1901, 372 pp.

Fay, Bernard
*Louis XVI: or The End of a World*
London, W.H. Allen, 1968, 414 pp.

Habsburg, Archduke Otto von
*Charles V*
New York, Praeger 1970, 258 pp.

Hughes, Philip
*A Popular History of the Reformation*
Garden City, Hanover House 1957, 343 pp.

Kelley, Francis C., Most Reverend
*Blood-Drenched Altars*
Rockford, IL, TAN Books, 502 pp.

Kurth, Godfrey
*The Church at the Turning Points of History*
Helena, MT, Naegele Printing Co. 1929, 192 pp.

Loewenstein-Scharffeneck, Hubertus, Prince zu
*The Germans in History*
New York, Columbia University Press 1945, 584 pp.

Mourret, SS., Fr. Fernand
*A History of the Catholic Church*
St. Louis, B. Herder 1958, 8 vols.

Neill, Thomas P.
*They Lived the Faith*
Milwaukee, Bruce Publishing Co., 1951, 388 pp.

Poulet, Dom Charles
*A History of the Catholic Church*
St. Louis, B. Herder 1950, 2 vols.

Slaves of the Immaculate Heart of Mary
*Our Glorious Popes*
Cambridge, MA., 1955, 183 pp.

Walsh, James Joseph
*The Thirteenth, Greatest of Centuries*
New York, AMS Press 1970, 400 pp.

Walsh, William Thomas
*Characters of the Inquisition*
Rockford, IL, TAN Books    1987

Walsh, William Thomas
*Phillip II*
London, Sheed & Ward 1937

Webster, Nesta
*The French Revolution*
London, Constable and Co., 1926, 519 pp.

## V. FICTION

Man does not live by bread alone, and all work and no play makes Jack a dull boy. Catholic sensibilities are not formed by facts alone, and all non-fiction and no literature makes Jack a dull Catholic. It is necessary for us to regain that sense of wonder that the Mechanistic society we live in robs us of. If we are not ashamed to quest for the Holy Grail, we will be ecstatic to drink of it at Mass. Thus the books here are wondrous, Catholic, and amusing. But they are only a few of the many awaiting you. Good Hunting!

Bernanos, Georges
*Diary of a Country Priest*
New York, Macmillan 1954, 298 pp.

Benson, Robert Hugh
*The King's Achievement*
London, Hutchinson and Co.

Benson, Robert Hugh
*Lord of the World*
New York, Dodd, Mead, and Co. 1906

Corvo, Frederick Rolfe, Baron
*Hadrian the Seventh*
New York, A.A. Knopf 1937, 350 pp.

Dante Aligheri
*The Divine Comedy*

Lewis, C.S.
*That Hideous Strength*
New York, Macmillan 1946, 459 pp.

Machen, Arthur
*Tales of Horror and the Supernatural*
New York, A.A. Knopf 1948, 427 pp.

Malory, Sir Thomas
*Le Morte d'Arthur*
New York, Charles Scribner's Sons, 1982, 750 pp.

Miller, Walter M.
*A Canticle for Leibowitz*
New York, J.B. Lippincott 1960, 320 pp.

Pegis, Anton Charles
*The Wisdom of Catholicism*
New York, Modern Library 1955, 988 pp.

Tolkien, J.R.R.
*The Hobbit*
Boston, Houghton Mifflin, 1966, 317 pp.

Tolkien, J.R.R.
*The Lord of the Rings*
Boston, Houghton Mifflin 1965, 3 vols.

Walsh, Thomas
*The Catholic Anthology, the World's Great Catholic Poetry*
New York, Macmillan, 1939, 584 pp.

Waugh, Evelyn
*Brideshead Revisited*
London, Chapman and Hall, Ltd. 1945, 304 pp.

Williams, Charles
*All Hallow's Eve*
London, Faber and Faber, 1960, 240 pp.

Williams, Charles
*War in Heaven*
London, Faber and Faber 1962, 256 pp.

## VI. PUBLICATIONS

It helps to stay abreast of things, and while there are many good Catholic publications, I here recommend only three. Not that the others are bad, but the first one will give all their addresses, and the last two are the primary news sources for the others.

Catholic Traditionalist Directory
Radko Jansky
7404 Zephr Pl.
Maplewood,
St. Louis, MO 63143

The Remnant
2539 Morrison Ave.
St. Paul, MN 55117

Christian Order
Rev. Paul Crane, SJ
65, Belgrave Rd.
London S.W.1V, 2BG Eng

The Wanderer
201 Ohio St.
St. Paul, MN 55107

# VII. ORGANIZATIONS

While reading does improve the mind, and individual effort is important, corporate action is most effective. The Organizations I mention here have different goals, and different methods of operation. Some would be upset at being listed on the same page with others. I myself do not agree entirely with some of them. But their hearts are all in the right place. We should remember the proverb, "In essentials, unity; in non-essentials, liberty; in all things, charity." In the directory listed above are many more, but your author cannot vouch for all of them. Let the buyer beware.

Catholic League for Religious & Civil Rights
Dr. Kevin Long
1100 W. Wells St.
Milwaukee, WI 53233

Catholic Traditionalist Movement
210 Maple Ave., P.O. Box 781
Westbury, L.I., New York 11590

Catholics United for Life
New Hope, KY 40052
Anti-abortion

Fidelity Forum
P.O. Box 5664
San Antonio, TX 78201
Monitors abuses

The Roman Forum
12 Indian Trail
West Milford, NJ 07480

St. Thomas More Educational Foundation
P.O. Box 44
Milwaukee, WI 53172

Society of St. Pius X
St. Thomas Aquinas Seminary
209 Tackora Trail
Ridgefield, CT 06877
Maintains Mass Centers, under Archbishop Lefebvre

TFP-American Society for Defence of Tradition, Family and Property
P.O. Box 121
Pleasantville, NY 10570
Political Action

Traditional Mass Society
P.O. Box 447
San Juan Capistrano, CA 92693
Works to extend Papal Indult

U.S. Tridentine Rite Conference
c/o Fr. Francis L. LeBlanc
8626 N. 106th Lane
Peoria, AZ 85345

Viva Il Papa
P.O. Box 4002
Portland, OR 97208

In addition, the Author welcomes correspondence:

Charles A. Coulombe
P.O. Box ~~771~~ 660771
Arcadia, CA ~~91006~~
91066